VALUE SEEKER
The Betting System

About the author

Anthony Gibson

I first took a minor interest in the sport of horse racing after my first ever bet won the 1965 Grand National. Jay Trump was my selection and won at the odds of 100/8. I was just ten at the time and I have been enthralled by every aspect of the sport ever since. Horse racing is now my full-time occupation and has been for quite some time. Not only do I earn money as a professional bettor, I also take time to post daily selections on my website from methods I continually devise and currently use to beat the bookies. Members of my site tend to be like-minded racing enthusiasts, who can take a long-term view to making profits. The ongoing research I perform generally throws up endless new betting angles and part of my success has been my ability to change with the times and adopt new methods and strategies. Since I went public on the site, all of the forums have continued to produce profits for members, which is no mean feat. Some of my members are still with me from day one since going live more than ten years ago.

I also enjoy writing educational articles for a number of different online monthly publications, on a variety of subjects relating to horse racing selection methods and betting. My objective is to try to educate my fellow punters in the art of using a disciplined approach and to try to encourage them to formulate strategies of their own in an attempt to beat their counterparts on the exchanges or the online and high street bookmakers. This makes for a very satisfying and interesting career although not one without its frustrations.

VALUE SEEKER
The Betting System

ANTHONY GIBSON

Published in 2015 by Raceform Ltd
27 Kingfisher Court, Hambridge Road, Newbury, Berkshire, RG14 5SJ

A catalogue record for this book is available from the British Library.

ISBN: 978-1-909471-96-2
EBOOK: 978-1-910498-26-2
KINDLE: 978-1-910498-25-2

Designed by Fiona Pike

Printed in the UK by Keeps Printing, Newbury

CONTENTS

Acknowledgements

I would like to thank *Racing Post* Books for allowing me the opportunity to get my name out to a wider audience and helping me to achieve a lifetime's ambition of producing a book on my favourite subject and to all who have had the foresight to purchase this book. I sincerely hope you make use of the information in this book and that the profits continue.

Note: The information in the book takes us to the end of December 2014. Up-to-date results can be obtained by email or are on display on my website and are updated on a monthly basis. I hope this is the start of future titles from me as an author.

INTRODUCTION

My alarm goes off in the early hours each morning, I take a look out of the window, it's raining heavily, it's going to be good to soft today, are the first thoughts that run through my brain. After getting showered and dressed I will collect my *Racing Post* from my local newsagent. The information I now hold in my hand will dictate whether I stand or fall, so on with the task of finding the day's selections.

Firstly I would like to point out that although this book takes a systematic approach to finding selections, it does not adhere to a rigid, black and white set of rules that must be followed at all costs. The selection method is based on my very simplistic approach to finding value bets each and every day racing takes place in the UK. The method normally finds a few what I regard as good value bets most days racing takes place. It is very rare that I have a no-bet day using this method.

Following a rigid set of rules, for example top weights in handicaps wearing blinkers for the first time, is all well and good and may provide you with some winners and a good profit, but there are times when you look at some of the selections a rigid system produces and deep down you know they don't really warrant a bet. This may be for many reasons, such as the ground may not suit, the course may not suit, or the trainer is out of form, yet you have to back it because the system rules make it a bet. This type of black and white, systematic approach does not interest me at all as generally this approach is flawed and has no real substance. Methods like these tend to make profits on a short-term basis then dry up and rack up losses. Generally the author has found a window of opportunity when the system has made money and sells it on while the results are hot. By the time you get hold of the system and put it into practice, that window of opportunity could be well and truly shut.

What I am offering in this book is a selection method that has some flexibility within the rules, yet still takes a systematic approach to finding selections using fluid statistics that change with the times. I like to use this method as it takes any sentiment out of betting if you follow my *modus operandi* to the letter. Basically you can find selections each morning. Place your bets and if you like, forget about the results until you check your betting bank the following day when you examine your profit or losses. The selections are arrived at using a simple set of rules based on strong statistics, a common sense approach with some basic form angles. We won't be following any newspaper tipsters although some are very good, but they can only express their view on a race using a deep knowledge of the sport. Having to make a selection in most races run on the day makes their task of finding winners almost impossible and unfortunately a good tipster will gain a following meaning the prices tend to shrink. I certainly do not take any notice of any so-called inside information having had my fingers burned far too many times listening to people on the inside of racing (for example, trainers and stable staff with elevated opinions of their own horses). I get texts now almost every single day from work riders, ex-jockeys, news from Ireland and so on. You almost have to feel sorry for the bookies with all of this good information about!

A systematic approach to selection using solid data is my method and that of many successful punters I have personally met and spoken to or read about. After all, we are dealing with sets of figures and statistics when trying to evaluate good form from bad. Trying to make some sense of the masses of statistics on a daily basis is not an easy task. My 'systematic approach' based on my simple idea of how to achieve value allied with other solid basic elements of form has produced magnificent profits to date and continues to do so. I am finding some very high-priced winners that seem to be overlooked by the masses, which is how a successful bettor operates. The price of some of the selections found using this method should not put you off backing them as the basis for making these a selection has very sound principles. We are not being influenced by anyone else when evaluating the selection's chances of winning. Basically if a selection falls into the method's criteria it's a bet regardless of price.

Trainers are the basis of my method, while other factors will also play a major role in whether I think a horse can win or not and make it a bet on the day. If the trainer has done his or her job and got the horse to the track both fit and well, the other factors I use mean it should run well on the day. These factors involve following trainers with a terrific strike rate at a particular course, trainers who on paper look to have a well handicapped or unexposed runner at a track where the statistics suggest the trainer looks to have lay out his or her horses to win the races at this course. When all of these elements come together then we have a terrific chance of winning our bet at much bigger odds than the statistics and betting suggest.

How to turn a set of statistics in your favour

The basis of my selection method is to look at reliable, strong statistics, and to use these favourable statistics to try and make a profit. There are of course statistics for everything these days but it is all about making use of the ones that are relevant. The example I am about to show you is not relevant to my selection method but is purely an example to show how a set of statistics can be used in your favour. Take a look at the following table which includes some of the top trainers in the UK today. The list shows trainers who have won more than one million pounds in prize money during the 2014 season.

Table from the start of the Flat turf racing in March to August 28, 2014

Trainer	Wins	Runs	%	£1 Staked	Value Bet
John Gosden	**93**	**429**	**22**	**-2.68**	**5.6**
Richard Hannon	151	962	16	-217.81	7.25
A P O'Brien	9	64	14	-23.44	8.2
Mark Johnston	185	1074	17	-116.13	7.0
Richard Fahey	142	1066	13	-132.85	8.7
Sir Michael Stoute	53	310	17	-125.24	7.0
William Haggas	**97**	**357**	**27**	**+80.33**	**4.8**
Roger Varian	65	349	19	-39.56	6.3
Marco Botti	67	453	15	-77.46	7.7
David O'Meara	94	541	15	-52.77	7.7
Andrew Balding	75	437	17	-41.80	7.0
Edward Lynam	**6**	**9**	**67**	**+14.50**	**2.5**
Kevin Ryan	54	498	13	-115.49	8.7

If you had set out a list of trainers to follow at the start of the Flat season and just by chance the trainers were the ones listed above, I think you would be rather disappointed from a punting point of view as you would be looking at a hefty loss backing their selections to a £1 level stake. In fact at this stage of the season you would be making quite a hefty loss of £850.40.

Of course at the start of the Flat season you would not set out to follow a list of trainers blindly to a £1 stake as this would always prove to be a bit of a mindless exercise as most do generally make a loss. However you only need to look at the previous year's table, whether it's Flat, National Hunt or all weather, to realise that more or less the same names appear there. Their positions may vary slightly from year to year, but the statistics remain fairly constant and form the basis of my actual method and it proves that some things in racing remain fairly consistent. Trainers may have a bad season from time to time but the good yards are pretty reliable. It's a fact that the top trainers always attract the owners who send the best horses and the best jockeys will be booked to ride them. Simple. Now if I had published the whole set of figures from the table, out of the 140 trainers listed there, only 31 are currently showing a profit. Note that I have added another column on the right, Value Bet. This is the crux of the method I am about to reveal to you in this book. So much is said about backing horses at value odds. Switch on your TV and watch *The Morning Line* and there may be some pundit on saying, 'this horse looks terrific value'. How does he or she know that? And how have they arrived at this assumption? I often look at these so-called 'value bets' to try to get my head around the subject and generally fail. What is value to one person may seem poor value to another.

Here is my simplistic approach to this matter of 'value'. If a trainer has a strike rate of 20 per cent then I would not want to be backing any of his horses on a long-term basis at under 5/1 (100 per cent divided by 20 per cent equals five). Anything above 5/1 (6.0 decimal odds shown in the table) would be more appealing with a view to making long-term profits. If you look at the column on the right you can see my rounded up decimal odds. These are the prices I would need to be taking to break even or better still, beat this figure before I would place a bet on any of the trainers' runners. This is my take on value as it is mathematically correct.

Another significant factor from the table is that if a trainer is hitting around the 20 per cent winner mark then it is likely he or she is going to be showing a long-term profit. Twenty per cent or above seems to be the magic number. So If we only concentrated on trainers who hit the 20 per cent minimum strike rate of winners (Gosden, Haggas and Lynam), the massive losses I spoke about following all trainers become quite an impressive turnaround into a profit of +92.15. The minimum 20 per cent strike rate has worked its magic.

I am looking at the figures above purely from a punting point of view. From an enthusiast's view I greatly admire all of the trainers on the list and their staff, plus the jockeys who put in so much hard work each and every day for our pleasure. It goes without saying, John Gosden in particular had an amazing season in 2014, netting more than 3.5 million in prize money and he managed to produce a very high strike rate to boot which shows the genius of the man. William Haggas also maintained a terrific strike rate all season for the amount of runners he sent out.

With respect to all trainers and their staff, the trainers who hit a 20 per cent and above strike rate at certain tracks up and down the country and produced a profit to level stakes, are the trainers you should be making your allies and the ones we should be following. These trainers generally look like their runners have turned up to win today's race and sometimes at good value prices. Whether it be on the Flat turf tracks, all weather or National Hunt, my method is sound and works all year round. I search out value bets allied to solid form on a daily basis and make huge profits in the process. You too can become a value seeking punter using this method and you will be astonished as to how easy this method is to implement.

THE SEARCH FOR VALUE

Having established that the whole crux of this method is to find good value bets on a daily basis and that following trainers with a minimum 20 per cent strike rate is the key to our success, I will now proceed to show you in as much detail as possible, how I arrive at my selections each day. I go through this process automatically each morning and it comes relatively easily to me and the process is precise, meaning there are no grey areas as to whether a particular horse is a selection or not.

The method is so simple that even on a day when there are five plus meetings it will take me no longer than ten minutes to go through all of the meetings on that day. I will aim to leave you in exactly the same position and each day your own selections should mirror my own. I apologise if at times some of the text is a little repetitive but as far as I know not all of my readers will have read or even seen a copy of the *Racing Post* before, let alone placed a bet. Therefore each process of the selection method and the art of placing a bet at the right price must be made clear. Also at the end of the book I will explain how further support and tuition are open to you should you require them.

With so many meetings these days and so much data printed each day in the racing press, it would be very difficult to go through each race at every meeting with a fine-tooth comb and be confident you had found a winner. I believe you must specialise in certain areas of data to cut down your workload, for example, race types, following jockeys, following trainers or following the money, or a little of each. Whatever you favour, try to gain some expertise in the area you are looking at to give yourself a chance of beating the book. We all know that there is too much low grade, uninspiring racing, especially during the week. Unfortunately it is the bookies who call the tune not the punters, and with the way racing is set up at present this scenario suits them fine, as this low-grade stuff generally throws up shock results. I personally at this moment in time follow three strategies, my value seeker being one of them. This may change some time in the future, but it is my value seeker method that is currently making me most money and this is the method this book is based on.

Value seeker follows trainers who have a high strike rate at certain courses. It is strange that some trainers may have a high strike rate at some tracks yet poor strike rates at others. I haven't quite grasped why this should be. You would think that a good trainer with a stable housing top quality horses would be able to replicate the high strike rate we are looking for across the county. Strangely enough they don't, some do come close though. The same goes for their runners at the tracks. Some trainers have terrific strike rates with two-year-olds and a poor return with their three-year-olds, or a good record with chasers and a poor one with hurdlers. The strike rate I look for at any course is a minimum of 20 per cent. The trainer must also have achieved this strike rate by having at least ten winners at the course to qualify. Therefore if a trainer has bang on 20 per cent winners at a course, he must have saddled 50 runners there yielding at least ten winners. The next rule is that they must also show a profit at the track to a £1 level stake. There is no point backing plenty of winners yet making an overall loss.

The table below shows trainers with runners at York on August 8, 2014

TRAINER	WINS-RUNS	£1 staked	%	2YO WINS RUNS	%	3YO WINS RUNS	%
Richard Fahey 3	46-611	-214.45	8	18-168	11	28-433	6
David O'Meara 1	28-231	-18.25	12	1-19	5	27-212	13
Kevin Ryan 7	25-220	-29.64	11	17-82	21	8-136	6
William Haggas 2	24-102	**+29.35**	**24**	6-23	**26**	18-79	**23**
Tim Easterby 2	22-340	-97.50	6	5-88	6	17-252	7
Sir Michael Stoute 2	15-76	-11.79	20	0-2	0	15-74	20
Michael Easterby 1	14-232	-98.50	6	3-58	5	11-174	6
Saeed Bin Suroor 1	12-116	-52.85	10	1-9	11	11-107	10
David Barron 4	12-126	-13.67	10	4-19	21	8-107	7
Mark Johnston 6	12-227	-153.40	5	6-65	9	6-162	4
Luca Cumani 1	11-58	**+10.00**	19	1-6	17	11-52	21
John Gosden 1	10-65	-8.87	15	0-4	0	10-61	16
Brian Ellison 7	10-126	**+3.50**	8	0-9	0	10-117	9
Roger Varian 1	6-39	**+2.23**	15	2-8	25	4-31	13
Paul Midgley 2	6-69	**+4.00**	9	0-13	0	6-56	11
Michael Dods 1	6-77	-9.50	8	1-14	7	5-63	8
David Nicholls 1	6-141	-76.50	4	0-9	0	6-132	5
Ronald Harris 3	5-44	**+33.00**	11	0-7	0	5-37	14
B W Hills 2	5-61	-12.25	8	2-22	9	3-39	8
John Quinn 1	5-86	-56.17	6	2-14	14	3-72	4
Sir Mark Prescott 1	4-18	**+17.07**	22	2-5	40	2-13	15
Ed Dunlop 3	4-36	-13.62	11	0-3	0	4-33	12
A P O'Brien 5	3-43	-26.75	7	0-13	0	3-30	10

TRAINER	WINS-RUNS	£1 staked	%	2YO WINS RUNS	%	3YO WINS RUNS	%
Tom Tate 1	3-55	-34.25	5	0-4	0	3-51	6
Richard Hannon 2	2-13	+18.00	15	0-4	0	2-9	22
Roger Charlton 2	2-23	-17.12	9	1-1	100	1-22	5
Robert Cowell 2	2-25	+33.00	8	0-2	0	2-23	9
Peter Chapple Hyam 2	2-27	+12.00	7	1-8	13	1-9	19
Charles Hills 3	2-38	-25.50	5	2-14	14	0-24	0
Brian Meehan 2	2-38	-31.62	5	1-15	7	1-23	4
Robert Eddery 1	1-3	+26.00	33	1-1	100	0-2	0
A J Martin 1	1-4	+5.00	25	0-0	0	1-4	25
K R Burke 2	1-8	-3.00	13	0-2	0	1-6	17
David Brown 1	1-28	-22.00	4	0-14	0	1-14	7
Alan Swinbank 1	1-38	-9.00	3	0-5	0	1-33	3
James Given 1	0-28	-28.00	0	0-5	0	0-23	0
Jamie Osborne 1	0-12	-12.00	0	0-1	0	0-11	0
Rod Millman 1	0-5	-5.00	0	0-3	0	0-2	0
James Moffatt 1	0-3	-3.00	0	0-0	0	0-3	0
John Spearing 1	0-1	-2.00	0	0-0	0	0-2	0
Tony Carroll 1	0-1	-1.00	0	0-0	0	0-1	0

Note: The source of my information to access these statistics is the *Racing Post*. Tables for trainers' records at each meeting are published in the Race Cards section. I do not know of anywhere else where such in-depth statistics are published.

To find possible selections we are looking for trainers who have had ten or more winners at the meeting. See the table below which shows the remaining possible qualifiers who fit this criteria:

TRAINER	WINS-RUNS	£1 staked	%	2YO WINS RUNS	%	3YO WINS RUNS	%
Richard Fahey 3	46-611	-214.45	8	18-168	11	28-433	6
David O'Meara 1	28-231	-18.25	12	1-19	5	27-212	13
Kevin Ryan 7	25-220	-29.64	11	17-82	21	8-136	6
William Haggas 2	**24-102**	**+29.35**	**24**	6-23	26	18-79	23
Tim Easterby 2	22-340	-97.50	6	5-88	6	17-252	7
Sir Michael Stoute 2	15-76	-11.79	20	0-2	0	15-74	20
Michael Easterby 1	14-232	-98.50	6	3-58	5	11-174	6
Saeed Bin Suroor 1	12-116	-52.85	10	1-9	11	11-107	10

TRAINER	WINS-RUNS	£1 staked	%	2YO WINS RUNS	%	3YO WINS RUNS	%
David Barron 4	12-126	-13.67	10	4-19	21	8-107	7
Mark Johnston 6	12-227	-153.40	5	6-65	9	6-162	4
Luca Cumani 1	11-58	**+10.00**	19	1-6	17	11-52	21
John Gosden 1	10-65	-8.87	15	0-4	0	10-61	16
Brian Ellison 7	10-126	**+3.50**	8	0-9	0	10-117	9

Of the 41 trainers on the master list we have straight away cut this down to the possible 13 trainers listed above. Our criteria for a trainer to qualify further is that he or she must have a minimum 20 per cent strike rate at the course and show a profit to a £1 level stake. Only William Haggas meets this criteria. Therefore from a meeting with 84 declared runners, we have immediately cut this down to just two trained by William Haggas who is the only trainer who fits our first criteria for selections.

TRAINER	WINS-RUNS	£1 staked	%	2YO WINS RUNS	%	3YO WINS RUNS	%
William Haggas 2	**24-102**	**+29.35**	**24**	6-23	26	18-79	23

Note: The figure after the trainer's name denotes how many runners he or she may have at the meeting. We must go through each race on the card searching for these runners and circle them when found. The number of runners is also significant when it comes to staking the selections, but more on this later in the book.

VALUE SEEKER: THE METHOD

I first started backing selections from the method after researching it thoroughly and had noted the success the trainers were having if fitting my criteria for selection. On July 1, 2013, I put a bank in place and started backing selections with hard cash and continue to do so to this day. There are not many so-called systems that stand the test of time but as I have previously stated my method is systematic in its approach to finding selections but is not black and white sticking to hard and fast rules. I don't think there can be a method that works for a long period of time based on a rigid formula, for the simple reason that racing itself is fluid. Jockeys and trainers come and go, jockey and trainer combinations that were once a potent combination part company for whatever reason. Jockeys hit highs and lows in their careers as do trainers. Also courses change configuration and there seems likely to be some new all-weather tracks planned pretty soon, bringing with them a whole new set of statistics. The rules of racing change and as with many other businesses, change is necessary and hopefully these changes are for the better.

My method is successful as it is based on strong statistics, statistics that change in tandem with the changes made above. The statistics I use are also allied to some basic but relevant form study and the combination is proving to be quite a potent force. The major plus is that we are backing horses at the right prices (the only way realistically to make money). It is very rare that I will bet on a horse less than 3/1 these days because of this method, generally my selections will almost certainly be around the 5/1 mark or much bigger. To do this and achieve the return on investment I have to date is quite phenomenal. This also means that the selections the method chooses are being ignored by tipsters and the general betting population or they would not be sent off at the prices that they are. The rules of the method may change again in the future, especially if I spot a trend that brings more winners to the table. Indeed you may spot something yourself after reading the book which may enhance the method — we must always be on the lookout for improvement.

Going back to the first table above showing trainers hitting the one million pound mark, I have established that trainers with a minimum 20 per cent rate generally show a profit. Surely the small bunch of trainers who manage to achieve this are the ones we should be following? Take a look at the table below:

	Wins	Runs	%	£1 level staked
Richard Hannon	151	962	16	-217.81
Mark Johnston	185	1074	17	-116.13
Richard Fahey	142	1066	13	-132.85

It is obvious that the above trainers achieve the prize money amassed to date using what I call a scattergun approach, with runners here, there and everywhere and at a glance you would want to ignore all runners from such stables as their return to level stakes and strike rate is poor. However it would be wrong to do so as there are courses where these trainers do show a level stakes profit and achieve the strike rate and criteria we are looking for. This proves that taking a selective approach and following trainers' course statistics rather than overall statistics is the way to go.

The Racing Industry

You may think it is strange that I am writing a small paragraph here on how part of the racing industry operates, but it is very relevant to our selection method. It was interesting watching an interview on *Channel 4 Racing* the other day in which a trainer stated, 'I have 150 horses in training this year, but most are exposed, ageing handicappers. I will be having a clear out at the end of the season and bringing in new blood.' Racing after all is an industry and all about making a profit. Any business that doesn't, ceases to exist.

A trainer is always looking for the next new superstar, a horse that will make a name for him or her and put them on the map, so that of course they can attract new owners, expand the yard and invest in better facilities, just like any other business. It is a harsh fact that a horse which may have served an owner/trainer well in its younger days, once it's over the top and not likely to win races in the future, will either be retired or sold on. The stars of the show — Group winners and Classic winners — will serve a long and happy retirement at stud, breeding the stars of the future. It is the young, unexposed horses a trainer has a chance to shine with and these types of horses are obviously where his or her future lies and where their likely future big race winners will come from. This being the case then surely this has to be the main area from which we source our likely winners too?

Exposed and unexposed explained

This leads me on to the next part of our method. If it is the unexposed horses that are the main source of any trainer's winners then that is the area we must concentrate on as punters. If you look at any trainer's or jockey's source of winners throughout a season, most will be unexposed types together with a few well handicapped runners. This statement is rather obvious when you think about it. Winners will generally come from horses which have not yet been assessed by the official handicapper. A horse with the most unexposed of profiles would be a two-year-old running for the first time in its life. Anyone who isn't involved in the horse's preparation has not got a clue what the horse is capable of producing on the track. You can of course look up its breeding for clues, how much the horse cost at the sales and future entries. The betting market may offer some clues too, but we still don't know how fit the horse is for its debut or how green the horse may be on the day.

My theory which the value seeker method is based on is this: if a trainer has a 25 per cent strike rate at a track and his debutant is quoted say 10.0 decimal odds (9/1), then that looks like a value bet to me as the trainer's horses should be around the 5.0 mark to still be a fair bet (100 per cent divided by 25 per cent equals four which is 4/1 industry points, 5.0 decimal odds) if we matched this to his or her strike rate. If we can beat the odds matched to the trainer's overall strike rate at the track then I would be having a bet on the horse regardless of its inexperience or any other factors that may deter many other punters from not having a bet as we have achieved value (on statistics alone).

If we can find bets like these on a day-in day-out basis (not all two-year-old debutants, but unexposed or well handicapped types) running at far bigger odds than the trainer's current overall strike rate at the track, we will win money in the long-term and my results to date prove this. A prime example of this and a recent winner was a Luca Cumani-trained two-year-old running for the first time at York. Its odds were 40.0 yet Cumani has an overall strike rate at York of 20 per cent so realistically the horse's odds should have been around the 6.0 mark (100 divided by 20 per cent equals 5/1 industry points, 6.0 decimal). I was very happy to take the 40.0 and watch it skate home. Another unbelievable fact about the price was that the horse was ridden by one of the country's top jockeys, Ryan Moore.

Establishing whether a horse is unexposed or exposed will come in time. The more you use this method and start to gain experience, the easier they will become to spot. I will go through a few examples below just to give you a bit of a grounding and I will also explain more as I go through the selection method itself.

Any horse that has not yet received a rating from the Official Handicapper can be considered unexposed. A horse can still be considered to be unexposed if a rating has been awarded (this is after three runs in public). A horse may have run three times in maidens, then first time in a handicap, be given a lowly rating by the assessor, then bang in it goes at big odds defying its initial handicap mark and making fools of us all. Basically the horse was unexposed and its initial handicap rating was too low and obviously way off the mark.

Flat racing unexposed types:
Two-year-olds running in maidens
Two-year-olds running in nurseries
Three-year-olds running in maidens
Three-year-olds running in handicaps for the first time

Jump racing unexposed types:
National Hunt Flat runners
Novice and maiden hurdle runners
Handicap hurdle debutants
Novice and maiden chase runners
Chase handicap debutants

When a horse moves into the handicap ranks it can become difficult to win with. The handicapper may have been harsh when initially assessing a horse's ability after it contested non-handicap races and given it an official rating which is possibly higher than it can cope with and therefore it finds life tough in handicaps. This particular horse would possibly run up a sequence of losses before the handicapper relented and lowered its rating to reflect its current ability, hence giving it a chance to win races from a now lower but competitive mark.

The other side of the coin are the horses a trainer may have plotted a handicap route for. Just say the horse has a staying pedigree (requires long distances to show its best form), it may have run in three five-furlong maiden races (the minimum trip a horse can contest) and obviously been outpaced and on the face of it run poorly. The handicapper may look at the horse's record and see it has been well beaten on all three occasions and give it a low rating to start life in handicaps. The trainer, who knew the horse could not possibly win over five furlongs, can now run it over the correct distance of, say, one mile two furlongs and the horse bolts in, showing its true ability. This is just a possible scenario of course. The handicapper would take a dim view of this and hike up the horse's official rating, the horse may struggle to win a race from now on and its true ability has been displayed for all to see and has now likely become exposed.

There are many scenarios to consider when looking for exposed or unexposed types of horses but again I use a simple set of rules that help me to get around this problem which has worked well to date. Experience using this method will point you to the right type of horses to bet on.

Handicapping briefly explained

A basic understanding of handicapping is very important for any punter thinking about making money from this game, as the vast majority of a day's racing is made up of such races. This is a brief guide into the principles of handicap races. Handicaps are races which bring together horses of varying levels of ability. The idea being that the better horses in the race carry more weight than the poorer horses. So in theory, all horses in a handicap have an equal chance of winning, if they all run to the best of their ability. A perfectly framed handicapped race would be one in which all contestants cross the line in a dead-heat.

The weight to be carried by a horse in a handicap is determined by the horse's Official Rating (OR). This is a figure given to every horse after one of the following happens: the horse wins a race; the horse loses three times and in at least one of these races the horse finishes in the first six positions. If it does not get a top six finish in the first three runs, then it must continue racing until it achieves a top six position before it receives an Official Rating.

Once the horse has its Official Rating, it can then contest a handicap race. Its Official Rating is used in calculating how much weight it will carry in a handicap race. The actual weight is in relation to the rest of the runners' ratings. Basically, the rating will relate to pounds in weight. This means that, for example, a horse with a rating of 55 will carry 10lbs less than a horse in the same race which is rated at 65.

Handicaps have different levels; races are classed as 1-2-3-4-5-6 with one being the highest class handicaps and six being the bottom grade handicaps. The horse's Official Rating will determine which grade of race it can enter. So, if after three runs a horse is given a rating of 55, it may, for example, contest a Class 6; a 46-60 handicap.

For the rest of the horse's career its rating will adjust according to how it performs. If it wins races its rating will increase, and it will have to contest better races. And if it loses, the rating will drop and it will stay contesting low-grade races.

Horses' ratings are assessed once a week by the handicapper, so it is possible for a horse to rattle up two or three wins in a week and be allowed to race off the same rating. The handicapper can only make the horse run with a penalty of 3, 5 or 7lbs, if it turns out quickly after a win. So although the handicapper would like to raise the horse perhaps by 10 or 14lbs the next time he reassesses, the trainer can unleash him again off what would be a lenient rating compared to what it will be a few days later.

As I have previously mentioned, some trainers exploit this to the full, such as Sir Mark Prescott, who regularly manages to get his horses to rattle up long winning sequences due to this rule.

Hopefully the above has given you a foothold on handicapping and how it works, but as I go through my selection process I will explain how relevant a horse's Official Rating is and how we treat this when deciding on making a horse a selection or not.

Gotcha

Looking through my *Racing Post* today, having circled all of my possible qualifiers, I have gone back to check on their handicap marks, and just thought I ought to add this section to show the type of horses we should avoid backing. The trainer in question is David O'Meara who has three qualifying runners at Ayr. His runner in the 4.10, Scoreline, is a perfect example of a horse that the handicapper has caught up with.

The trainer qualified having the required 20 per cent strike rate and showing a profit to a £1 level stake and had more than ten winners at the course. The horse was also quoted around 7.0 (6/1) in the early morning markets, but as the horse was running in a handicap I had to do further investigations into its form as we do not have a bet on prices alone. You can get the lifetime form on the Racing Post website www.racingpost. com. In this case you could see that the horse was penalised for a win on June 14 and its Official Rating (these are the ratings I use not *Racing Post* Ratings) had gone up from 60 to 66. It then ran eighth at Leicester but bounced back with a win at Musselburgh. The handicapper raised its mark to 68, it managed to finish second from this new high mark, so the handicapper stepped in again and raised it to 71. From this new high mark the horse has finished sixth, eighth and recently fourth, beaten six lengths, 4.25 lengths and 4.5 lengths respectively. My view is that the horse is now struggling from its current rating so therefore not to be considered a betting proposition and therefore must be left alone. The handicapper has gotcha!

Flat placings 7268-22158142684

As you can see the horse has had a consistent profile for the first part of the season (22158142). Is it the new high mark that is causing the present inconsistency 684? I think so. The table below shows its lifetime form and ratings.

	FORM	WINS	MY RATINGS	STATISTICS	ENTRIES	RELATIVES	SALES	QUOTES				

	DATE	RACE CONDITIONS	WGT	RACE OUTCOME	JOCKEY	OR	TS	RPR
▣	30Sep14	Wol 6St C5Hc 2K	9-5	4/13 (4½L Thataboy 9-5) 14/1	Sam James	70	—	67
▣	17Sep14	Bev 5GF C5Hc 3K	9-4	8/9 (5¼L Ambitious Icarus 9-6) v¹ 5/1	Daniel Tudhope	71	51	59
▣	05Sep14	Mus 5Gd C5Hc 3K	8-13	6/9 (6L Noble Asset 9-4) p 6/1	Sam James	71	30	57
▣	15Aug14	Ncs 5GS C53yHc 2K	9-7	2/9 (½L Lucky Times 8-12) 11/2	Daniel Tudhope	68	56	73
▣	09Aug14	Ayr 5GS C63yHc 2K	9-7	4/6 (3L Autumn Tide 7-13) 7/2	Sam James	68	42	63
▣	01Aug14	Mus 5GF C6Hc 3K	9-4	1/6 (¾L Tadalavil 8-9) 4/1	Sam James	63	50	71
▣	05Jul14	Lei 5GF C53yHc 3K	9-3	8/11 (11L The Dandy Yank 9-7) 4/1	Ben Curtis	65	26	33
▣	11Jun14	Ham 5Sft C63yHc 2K	9-6	5/6 (3L Tinsill 9-7) 7/2	Julie Burke	66	32	59
▣	05Jun14	Sth 5St C53yMd 2K	9-5	1/6 (shd Epic Voyage 9-5) 11/10F	Daniel Tudhope	60	64	74
▣	28May14	Ham 5Gd C6Hc 2K	9-2	2/9 (1½L Raise A Billion 8-1) 3/1F	Daniel Tudhope	60	52	65
▣	19May14	Red 5GF C63yHc 1K	9-7	2/12 (2¼L Storyline 9-5) 7/1	Daniel Tudhope	60	57	65
▣	08Oct13	Cat 6GS C62yHc 2K	9-7	8/11 (7¼L Signore Piccolo 9-3) 8/1	David Nolan	65	17	45
▣	19Sep13	Pon 5Gd C52yMd 3K	9-5	6/8 (7½L Omaha Gold 9-0) 9/2	David Nolan	—	39	51
▣	10Sep13	Red 5Sft C62yMdAc 2K	9-1	2/11 (1L White Flag 8-1) 11/4F	Daniel Tudhope	—	47	62
▣	06May13	Bev 5GF C62yMd 2K	9-5	7/9 (16L Zalzilah 9-5) 7/2	Daniel Tudhope	—	—	23

Full Result							
Pos	Dist	Horse	Trainer	Age	Weight	Jockey	SP
1ˢᵗ (5)		5 Fredricka	G Moss	3	9-4	Jason Hart	10/3
2ⁿᵈ (7)	2	2 Margrets Gift	T D Easterby	3	9-7 p	D Allan	13/8f
3ʳᵈ (8)	nk	3 Scoreline	D O'Meara	3	9-7 p	D Tudhope	6/1
4ᵗʰ (6)		6 Red Forever	A Berry	3	9-0	P Mathers	7/1

The above result of the 4.10 at Ayr shows that the horse we swerved, Scoreline, was a fairly well beaten but gallant third, hence saving us a point in our betting bank simply by doing a little research to see if the horse has an exposed or unexposed profile. Truly exposed, in the above example.

Selection process explained

I will now go into the full details of how to make your daily selections. The process for me is quite simple and even on a busy day with several meetings it will take me no longer than ten minutes to have my selections marked off for the day's racing. I achieve this is of course because I have the rules firmly fixed in my head. This is something that will also become second nature to you with practice. I will however go into as much detail as I think is necessary so even a beginner should grasp the method. The best way for me do this is to go through a full week's racing. The week I have chosen is Ebor week at York which has notoriously big fields and is a bit of a nightmare for punters. I will also cover all other meetings at the minor courses held throughout the week as well.

Basic system rules

The trainer must boast a minimum 20 per cent strike rate at the course and show a profit to a £1 level stake. The strike rate must be achieved by having at least ten winners to date at the course we are looking at. The final selection must ideally be an unexposed, lightly raced type, but if the possible selection is an older horse it must not be in the handicapper's grip as shown in our 'gotcha' example above.

If the horse is running in a handicap I will allow a horse 5lbs of improvement. For example, if a horse has won from an Official Rating of 80 and is still running into a place from this mark, and in today's race it is running off 85 then I will back it (5lbs higher). If a horse has been raised from 80 to 86 or above I will not back it regardless of its current form. Five pounds is the maximum penalty I will consider, anything above regardless of its current form, I will not back.

Simple enough basic rules but anomalies occur when applying any set of rules. This is why I class this as a selection method rather than a black and white system with rules that must be adhered to. The reader must at times apply his or her own logic when assessing the basic rules as sometimes the rules may not fit the puzzle the method dictates. I will try to explain in detail when such anomalies occur and how I tackled them, both in the following guide through the selections of a week's racing, and at the end of the book. I back all selections on the Betfair site www.betfair.com, always taking Betfair SP which I will explain in detail later.

I will also explain how you can get help and support on a day-to-day basis using my website or contacting me with any problems via email.

A WEEK'S RACING

Monday, August 18

Today we have meetings at Thirsk, Windsor, Kempton, and Wolverhampton.

Thirsk (Flat Turf)

As discussed, the main rule of the system is that we only look at trainers who have a minimum 20 per cent strike rate at the course who show a level stakes profit to a £1 bet and who must have had at least ten winners at the track. We have no trainers who meet the criteria at Thirsk today, so no bets.

Windsor (Flat Turf)

We have two qualifying trainers.

TRAINER	WINS-RUNS	£1 staked	%	2YO WINS RUNS	%	3YO WINS RUNS	%
Roger Varian 1	18-58	+28.75	31	1-8	13	17-50	34
Saeed Bin Suroor 1	12-42	+27.30	29	1-3	33	11-39	28

Both trainers fit our criteria and both trainers have one runner (the figure after the trainer's name. I will again explain the significance of this when it comes to staking selections).

It is here we take a further look at the trainers' statistics for the course. Bin Suroor has a 33 per cent strike rate with his two-year-old runners and a 28 per cent strike rate with his three-year-old runners. Varian has only a 13 per cent strike rate with his two-year-old runners (albeit from a fairly small sample of runners, just eight to date). Give the trainer the benefit of the doubt in a case like this as his overall strike rate is very good. I would recommend a trainer has at least ten runners in a category before you dismiss his runner, but we do need to look at trainers' records in each category as they can vary and some trainers seem to have good records in one and not the other. Ideally we want to see a minimum 20 per cent strike rate.

We must now check the horse's profile. Is it exposed and therefore no bet, or unexposed and a betting proposition? Saeed Bin Suroor's horse, Romance Story, runs in the 5.30, a two-year-old maiden. The horse has only run twice, so must qualify as being unexposed.

If this horse fits our next criteria on price then this is the type of horse I would consider to be a good value bet based on my calculation using the trainer's overall strike rate at the course. This calculation is 100 divided by his 29 per cent strike rate equals 3.45, so around a decimal price of 4.45 or above is ideally what we require to make this a bet.

Roger Varian's horse, Keepers Ring, runs in the 7.30, a three-year-old maiden race. The horse has only run once, so again must qualify as being unexposed. The trainer has a 31 per cent overall strike rate. The calculation here is 100 divided by 31 equals 3.23, so a decimal price of around 4.23 or above is ideal to be a value bet.

Kempton (Flat Turf)

We have three qualifying trainers who fit our criteria (20 per cent and above strike rate at the course plus a £1 level stakes profit at the course).

TRAINER	WINS-RUNS	£1 staked	%	2YO WINS RUNS	%	3YO WINS RUNS	%
Saeed Bin Suroor 2	59-214	+41.91	28	30-72	43	28-142	20
James Fanshawe 3	55-231	+85.09	24	1-22	5	54-209	26
Charlie Appleby 1	19-88	+14.66	22	10-53	19	9-35	26

Saeed Bin Suroor's first horse, Waghah, runs in the 2.30, an open-aged handicap race. Now handicaps must be treated differently to maidens as the horse must have an Official Rating to compete in a handicap, so we must look through the horse's form to see if we consider this runner exposed or unexposed. Remember my golden rule — I do not like horses that have been penalised for a previous win with more than 5lbs. We know that a horse's ability is expressed in pounds as I have briefly touched on earlier and a 5lb penalty is not insurmountable for a horse on the upgrade. This is the ceiling I set and stick to, a horse raised more than 5lbs is not considered betting material. The table below outlines Waghah's form.

Placings: 5-5130

OR 80	Starts	1st	2nd	3rd	Win & Pl
All Weather	1	1	—	—	£2,760
All Flat races	5	1	—	1	£3,458

5/14 Ling 1m 2f Class 5 maiden (AW) £2,760

The horse has an unexposed look having only run five times. If you look at the form in the *Racing Post* it won a maiden race in May at Lingfield. It was then given an Official Rating (OR) of 80 in two subsequent runs in handicaps. The horse's rating has remained the same at 80. If the horse's rating had gone up to 86, I would not have backed it. If the horse's rating had gone up to 85 then I would have backed it. So seeing as the handicapper has left the horse alone I am prepared to make this a bet as its profile is still relatively unexposed and likely to still have some improvement, especially on a surface which it hasn't encountered before.

If this horse fits our next criteria on price, it is a value bet. Based on my calculation using the trainer's strike rate at the course, we have a bet — the trainer has a 28 per cent overall strike rate, but a 33 per cent strike rate with his two-year-old runners. Take the trainer's overall strike rate to calculate the price required for selection. The calculation is 100 divided by 28 equals 3.57, so a decimal price of 4.57 or above is what we are looking for.

In the second race, the 3.00 at Kempton, two of the qualifying trainers have three runners (Fanshawe has two and Bin Suroor has one). I will have a bet in a race with two runners from our list of qualifying trainers, but when there are three or above I leave the race alone.

I have a rule that I put a line through any race that is contested by three or more horses from my qualifying trainers. The reason I will not back three horses in the same race is that apart from it looking too competitive, there can only be one winner and it may not come from any of our selected trainers' qualifying runners, hence possibly making us a hefty minimum loss of three points.

Charlie Appleby's runner in the 3.30, Winter Queen, was running in a nursery for the first time after qualifying with an Official Rating of 56 after finishing fourth, tenth, and ninth in its three maiden runs (today is only its fourth outing). Although unexposed and fitting our criteria, the horse was too short a price to warrant a bet.

James Fanshawe has the final runner of the meeting in the 5.30. He's My Boy is running in a three-year-old handicap so our first check is the horse's rating for qualification.

HE'S MY BOY					
Placings: 749-850741					
OR65	Starts	1st	2nd	3rd	Win & Pl
All Weather	3	—	—	—	£192
All Flat races	9	1	—	1	£4,314

57 8/14   NmkJ 6f Class 5 57-75 3yo Hcap gd-fm

If you take a look at the horse's record to date you can see it has run nine times, winning a six-furlong Class 5 handicap for three-year-old horses rated 57-75 last time out at Newmarket with an Official Rating of 57 (a clever bit of placing by this shrewd trainer getting the horse into this handicap of the lowest rating). The handicapper has decided to put the horse's rating up to 65 for today's race which is plus 8lbs (my cut off is above 5lbs) so the horse does not qualify.

Another note on James Fanshawe, his record with his three-year-old runners is outstanding. I have made lots of money following his three-year-old runners at today's course. But his two-year-old-runner record of just one winner from 22 runners is a poor five per cent strike rate. You would not be looking at the trainer's two-year-old runners for a bet with such a poor strike rate, remember 20 per cent and above.

Wolverhampton (Flat All Weather)

We have two qualifying trainers.

TRAINER	WINS-RUNS	£1 staked	%	2YO WINS RUNS	%	3YO WINS RUNS	%
Mike Murphy 1	21-91	+12.27	23	0-3	0	21-88	24
Ralph Beckett 1	16-71	+8.12	24	4-28	14	12-43	28

Although both trainers have an overall qualifying strike rate, we must look at each category separately (strike rate with two-year-old and three-year-old runners). Ralph Beckett has just the one runner at the course today, a two-year-old in a nursery which has an unexposed look. However if you look at the trainer's record at the track he has an overall strike rate of 24 per cent. His strike rate with three-year-old runners is 28 per cent, yet with his two-year-old runners is only 14 per cent and this comes from a fair amount of runners (28). In a case like this I dismiss his two-year-old runners at the track as his record is below what we are looking for (20 per cent plus). For whatever reason, his two-year-old runners do not perform well at this particular course.

Mike Murphy hasn't had a two-year-old winner, but he has only had three runners to date which is not enough to judge him on. If a trainer has had ten runners in a category and has not hit our 20 per cent and above strike rate, then we can dismiss his or her runners even though their overall strike rate may be 20 per cent and above. Taking a closer look at Murphy's two-year-old runner, it was beaten a big distance on debut (its only run to date) and is 50.0 in the betting market on Betfair. It doesn't look like a winner waiting to happen to me, so in both of the above cases I will not be having a bet.

To reiterate, when assessing the horse's price for value, you must take a trainer's overall per cent strike rate. Look at the trainer's record in each individual category as the trainer may have a good strike rate with his or her two-year olds but a poor record with three-year-olds or vice versa. The same applies for National Hunt racing where a trainer may have a good record with hurdlers but a poor record with chasers or vice versa.

Tuesday August 19

There are meetings at Brighton, Worcester, Leicester and Yarmouth.

Brighton (Flat Turf)

We have two qualifying trainers.

TRAINER	WINS-RUNS	£1 staked	%	2YO WINS RUNS	%	3YO WINS RUNS	%
David Simcock 2	18-48	+25.37	38	7-14	13	11-34	34
Mark Johnstone 1	15-68	+11.10	22	3-17	18	12-51	24

Mark Johnstone's runner, Mambo Rhythm, running in a three-year-old handicap with an unchanged Official Rating of 64, qualifies (unexposed).

David Simcock's runner, Patronella, again running in a three-year-old handicap with an unchanged Official Rating of 52 qualifies. His other runner, Hierarch, is totally exposed having run 52 times. It did however finish second last time out from a rating of 67 and is rated 69 today, within our 5lb limit. But even though the horse has won from a rating of 69 you have to go back to October 2010 for that win, so cannot be backed with any confidence. Note again here that you can go through a horse's lifetime form at www.racingpost.co.uk. It is well worth spending this extra time on research for the handful of qualifiers you may have on the day.

Worcester — National Hunt

We have three qualifying trainers.

TRAINER	WINS-RUNS	£1 staked	%	CHASES WINS RUNS	%	HURDLES WINS RUNS	%	NH FLAT
Paul Nicholls 1	47-248	+8.30	34	9-33	27	12-26	46	1-6
Charlie Longston 1	14-69	+5.96	20	7-27	26	2-28	7	5-14
Lawney Hill 1	12-53	+75.00	23	6-18	33	6-29	21	0-6

Now we have a chance to take a look at our first National Hunt meeting and note how the table changes from the Flat racing table. We have three categories — chases, hurdles and National Hunt Flat. Again we must find trainers who have a 20 per cent and above strike rate and show a £1 level stakes profit at the course for our selections. Note the trainers' runners per cent record in each category — in the National Hunt Flat column there are no per cent figures quoted, this you must work out for yourself. But these types of races are not a good betting medium and I would only follow trainers who have had ten winners or above in this sphere and the 20 per cent plus strike rate, which basically rules out most runners in this section anyway.

Treat selections exactly as you would on the Flat, but note that horses that win novice events are penalised for a win, but can still contest novice events (unlike maidens on the Flat). For example, a horse may win a novice event carrying a weight of 10st 12lbs, the next time it runs it will probably have been penalised 7lbs, so have to carry 11st 5lbs (up 7lbs) which is above our limit of 5lbs. So be very careful in novice events over the jumps as horses are penalised for winning but have not yet achieved an Official Rating. You must check if a horse has a penalty for a win, the same goes for novice chases and National Hunt Flat races.

It will not take you long to do this extra bit of research from the handful of qualifiers we have each day. Basically a novice winner over the jumps may well be penalised out of being a selection next time, but check in the horse's form to confirm this. Also be wary of horses moving from National Hunt Flat into novice events that may have won a race, but are unpenalised, as it is a totally different sphere as is hurdles to chases. See example below:

Jack Frost
Race record
4-y-o (10Feb10 ch g)

LIKE, SHARE, COMMENT **f** *Get involved* **RACING POST**

Midnight Legend (13.3f) — Bella Macrae (Bustino (11.3f))
Trainer **Nicky Henderson**
Owner **The Queen**
Breeder **The Queen**

+ ADD TO MY HORSE TRACKER

RACE RECORD PEDIGREE MY NOTES PHOTOS

Jumps placings 1115

LIFETIME RECORD	STARTS	WINS	2NDS	3RDS	WINNINGS	EARNINGS	BEST TS	BEST RPR	OR†
NHF	2	2	0	0	£4,310	£4,310	41	117	—
Hurdle	2	1	0	0	£3,899	£3,899	105	125	—
Rules Races	4	3	0	0	£8,209	£8,209	—	—	—

FORM WINS MY RATINGS STATISTICS ENTRIES RELATIVES SALES QUOTES

	DATE	RACE CONDITIONS	WGT	RACE OUTCOME	JOCKEY	OR	TS	RPR
▶	17Dec14	**Nby 19Sft** C4NvH 3K	11-2	5/10 (55L Value At Risk 10-12) 3/1	Peter Carberry	—	43	—
▶	24Nov14	**Lud 16GS** C4MdH 3K	10-11	**1/16** (3½L Father Edward 11-0) 1/2F	Peter Carberry	—	105	125
▶	06Nov14	**Fak 16GS** C6NHF 1K	11-8	**1/6** (3½L Thunder And Rain 10-11) 5/6F	Peter Carberry	—	41	117
▶	11May14	**Lud 16Gd** C5NHF 2K	10-11	**1/7** (1¼L Magnimity 11-0) 5/4F	Peter Carberry	—	12	96

Jack Frost, trained by Nicky Henderson, started life running in a NHF (National Hunt Flat) race at Ludlow, which it won carrying 10st 11lbs. The next race it contested was a NHF at Fakenham carrying 11st 8lbs — up 11lbs, no bet for us at it would have exceeded our 5lbs plus rule.

The trainer then decided to send the horse hurdling. As you can see it ran in a maiden hurdle back at Ludlow on November 24, in a new sphere and the weight back down to 10st 11lbs, a race which it won. The next time it ran in a novice hurdle the horse had to carry 11st 2lbs (plus 5lbs). This would be a bet for us if considering the penalty only, but not actually a bet on the day as the trainer's strike rate at the track is below 20 per cent. Note that the horse has not been assessed for an Official Rating yet.

Now back to our runners for the day's racing. Charlie Longston's runner, Long Wave, runs in a novice handicap chase. Its last run in a chase was from an Official Rating of 105. Today it runs off 114 (plus 9lbs) so no bet (I treat both Flat and National Hunt the same with up to 5lbs on its last rating to qualify as a bet). This also does not qualify on price.

Lawney Hill's runner, El Torreros runs in a novice handicap chase. Its last run was off 91 and today it runs off 99, no bet.

Paul Nicholls' runner, Merrion Square, runs in a novice hurdle. It has been penalised 5lbs for winning a handicap chase and has an official rating of 130 if it contests handicaps again. But today that penalty does not count back in novice company over hurdles, however it still does not qualify on price. Again be wary with selections over the jumps, trainers will switch runners from chases to hurdle races or vice versa to exploit a horse's favourable rating.

Leicester (Flat Turf)

We have two qualifying trainers.

TRAINER	WINS-RUNS	£1 staked	%	2YO WINS RUNS	%	3YO WINS RUNS	%
Luca Cumani 1	12-47	**+3.23**	26	1-16	13	10-31	**32**
William Haggas 1	10-36	**+17.95**	28	3-12	25	7-24	**29**

The Luca Cumani runner Endless Credit does not qualify on price.

The William Haggas runner Picture Postcard runs in a two-year-old maiden race, first time out so is totally unexposed and qualifies on price.

Yarmouth (Flat Turf)

We have one qualifying trainer.

TRAINER		WINS-RUNS	£1 staked	%	2YO WINS RUNS	%	3YO WINS RUNS	%
Chris Wall	1	27-128	**+13.53**	**21**	0-13	0	27-115	**23**

The Chris Wall runner Eleusis is an exposed two-year-old but the trainer's record at the track (0-13) makes this a no bet.

Wednesday, August 20

Today we have meetings at York, Musselburgh, Lingfield, Kempton and Southwell.

Musselburgh (Flat Turf)

We have three qualifying trainers Richard Fahey (1), Philip Kirby (2) and Alan Swinbank (3).

The Fahey runner did not qualify, running in a handicap off 7lbs higher than last time.

Both Kirby runners qualified, both running in handicaps and both penalised for wins, Stopped Out +1, and Rocky Two +4. Both are still fairly unexposed runners and both had won off higher marks in the past.

All three Swinbank runners were penalised for handicap wins — Entihaa +4, In Focus +8, Giovanni Jack +11, so just the one qualifier Entihaa who still looked fairly exposed.

Lingfield (Flat All Weather)

We have three qualifying trainers John Gosden (2), Robert Mills (1) and Daniel Mark Loughnane (1).

One Gosden runner did not qualify on price, the other qualified first time in a handicap and on price. Robert Mills's runner qualified first time in a handicap and Daniel Mark Loughnane's only runner qualified running in a handicap off its initial Official Rating.

Kempton (Flat Turf)

We have five qualifying trainers: James Fanshawe (3), Ralph Beckett(1), Saeed Bin Suroor (2) Kevin Ryan (1) and Charlie Appleby (3).

In the second race on the card, the 6.50 maiden, three of the qualifying trainers — Appleby, Fanshawe and Bin Suroor — had runners so I strike a line through the race. As mentioned earlier, we do not bet in races with three or more qualifying trainers competing.

In the next race, the 7.20 Maiden, Appleby had two runners that were unexposed but did not qualify on price.

In the next, the 7.50 handicap, both Ryan and Fanshawe had a runner. Both qualified as first time in a handicap and both qualified on price.

In the 8.50 handicap, Fanshawe had a runner that qualified, first time in a handicap and on price.

In the 9.20 handicap, Bin Suroor and Beckett both had runners. Beckett's did not qualify on price. Bin Suroor's was first time in a handicap and qualified on price.

York (Flat Turf)

We have one qualifying trainer, William Haggas (2).

In the 3.40 Group 1, Mukhadram qualifies. Its initial Official Rating of 122 remains unchanged and it is still unexposed.

In the 4.55 nursery handicap, Roossey qualifies as first time in a handicap.

Thursday, August 21

Today we have meetings at Ffos Las, Bath, Wolverhampton, York, and Newton Abbott.

Ffos Las (National Hunt)

We have one qualifying trainer, Anthony Honeyball.

TRAINER	WINS-RUNS	£1 staked	%	CHASES WINS RUNS	%	HURDLES WINS RUNS	%	NH FLAT
Anthony Honeyball 2	10-37	+18.66	27	4-7	57	1-16	6	5-14

If you look at the trainer's record at the track he obviously targets his chasers here as his wins-to-runs record is excellent at 27 per cent. His record with his hurdlers is not so good with just one winner from 16 runners and a very poor six per cent. His wins-runs ratio for his NHF runners (five from 14 which is 35 per cent) again is excellent.

My way of dealing with the above data is to obviously back his chasers if they have an unexposed profile or are well handicapped for today's race. Ignore his hurdlers as he has a good sample of runners to date, 16 with only the single winner. His National Hunt Flat runners have a great strike rate, but as I have previously stated this is not a medium I like to have a bet in as there are normally too many unexposed runners in this type of race and not a lot of form to go on. However if the trainer did have a double figure winners' record and a 20 per cent or above strike rate, then I would have had a bet on his runner if the price was right. I think you will find that trainers who do qualify with runners in this sphere with their per cent strike rate to runners, generally fail on price.

Today both the Honeyball runners are in hurdle races so no bet.

Bath (Flat Turf)

We have one qualifying trainer, Clive Cox (1). His only runner Shades Of Grey is running off a lower OR than its last win.

SHADES OF GREY					
Placings: /54451127/677045-275					
OR66	Starts	1st	2nd	3rd	Win & Pl
Turf	26	3	4	1	£ 11,986
All Flat races	39	3	4	1	£11,986

72 7/12 Newb 1m3f Class 5 56-75 App H'cap soft

66 7/12 Newb 1m3f Class 5 51-70 App H'cap gd-sft

63 10/11 Newb 1m4f Class 5 61-75 Am H'cap gd-fm

Although the horse could be well handicapped today (has won off 72, today runs off 66), if you look at its form the last time, it was placed second was from a mark of 65. However, in the horse's last ten runs it has been placed once (second) from this mark, which is 1lb lower than today's Official Rating, having posted form figures of 7/677045-275. Also it is two years since the horse won. This has the look of a thoroughly exposed handicapper so no bet on this one for me today. It pays to do your research before you place a bet.

Wolverhampton (All Weather)

We have three qualifying trainers George Baker (2), Mike Murphy (1) and Ralph Beckett (3).

Beckett's first runner on the card is making its debut in a handicap so qualifies (unexposed).

His second runner on the card runs in a maiden race along with the two George Baker runners, so here we have three qualifying trainers' runners in one race so we put a line through the race as I consider such races too competitive.

Beckett's third runner runs in the 9.20 race, again a maiden, and although the horse has run six times now and is starting to look exposed, it did however run well in a handicap last time out and must be given a chance back in this weak-looking maiden.

In the same race is the Mike Murphy runner which has only run once. The horse qualifies as it has only run once and is therefore unexposed using the rules of the system, but it was a well beaten 66/1 shot when last seen 258 days ago and is quoted 350.0 on the Betfair site. I am going to take a chance and watch this one run as I get the feeling that tonight will not be its moment of glory. The horse was beaten about 20 lengths. I must state here that it is dangerous to write any horse off that comes from one of our qualifiers, but it was clear in this case that the horse has not shown any ability to date and was a no hoper according to its starting price. The trainers we are following with this method are clearly not mugs and I don't think they would be allowing a horse with a chance to go off at a 350.0 starting price. As I stated earlier, the prices of the selections don't usually put me off having a bet, but this was way, way too big.

York (Flat Turf)

We have two qualifying trainers William Haggas (5) and Luca Cumani (1).

On the previous day's big meeting at York, only William Haggas had qualifiers at the course. Even though Luca Cumani had runners yesterday he did not qualify as his percentage of winners to runners was too low (19 per cent), but he had a winner which elevated him up to the magic 20 per cent mark, so today he is a qualifying trainer, as he also shows a level stakes profit. This proves that the statistics we are following are fluid and move with the times.

William Haggas has two runners in the first race which is a stakes race for two-year-olds and both horses are totally unexposed. He also has two runners in a Listed race, one has a rating today of 99 and its previous rating was 86 (plus 13) so does not qualify as a bet. His other runner has achieved a rating of 93 and has only run four times. Its mark is unchanged for today's race, so is a bet.

Luca Cumani's only runner ran off 80 two runs ago and is now rated 109, a whopping plus 29, so does not qualify for a bet today.

Friday, August 22

Today we have meetings at Ffos Las, Newmarket, Hamilton, Newcastle, York and Goodwood.

Ffos Las (National Hunt)

We have one qualifying trainer David Simcock (1).

GRAMERCY					
Placings: /0400316030-05503404					
OR85	Starts	1st	2nd	3rd	Win & Pl

Although the Simcock runner looks fairly well handicapped today running off 85 (has won off 92) the horse has an exposed look to it and you have to go back a year to the horse's last win. Basically the handicapper looks to be giving the horse a chance but I am overlooking its chances as it has not shown any worthwhile form for a while and could be regressing. I am a little worried that it is the trainer's only runner at the track though, but I am going to make it a no bet.

Newmarket

We have no qualifying trainers.

Hamilton (Flat Turf)

We have two qualifying trainers Kevin Ryan (2) and Mark Johnston (3).

Kevin Ryan's first runner is first time in a nursery (two-year-old handicap) so qualifies. His second runner has an initial Official Rating of 57 which remains unchanged and is unexposed so a bet.

Mark Johnston's first two runners are in the same race which is a Class 3 handicap. One runner has been raised 5lbs for a previous win and is still only a three-year-old so is fairly unexposed. His other runner has been raised from 78 to 90 (plus 12lbs) so does not qualify. His last runner on the card is running in the three-year-old maiden race, but has run eight times showing poor form and now looks exposed.

Newcastle

We have no qualifiers.

York (Flat Turf)

We have two qualifying trainers William Haggas (4) and Luca Cumani (2).

William Haggas's first runner is a three-year-old running first time in a handicap. His second runner, also a three-year-old, is running in a Listed race. Its initial rating of 104 remains the same today. His third runner is a two-year-old first time out and his fourth runner a three-year-old running in a handicap for the second time with an unchanged rating of 82. So all look unexposed and all will be bets.

Luca Cumani's first horse runs in an open-aged handicap and has been raised 5lbs for winning last time out, so qualifies for a bet, the horse does look very progressive. His second runner creates a bit of an anomaly again for us (as explained below). Remember we are not following hard and fast rules for selection and at times common sense must prevail. Experience using the method is also advantageous.

TRAINER	WINS-RUNS	£1 staked	%	2YO WINS RUNS	%	3YO WINS RUNS	%
Luca Cumani 2	12-60	+11.50	20	0-6	0	12-54	22

The trainer has a record at the track of 20 per cent which he only managed to achieve the previous day, so you could say that his strike rate is progressing with the more runners he sends to this course, so he obviously targets this track. His winners have come from his three-year-old runners (12-54). He has not yet had a two-year-old winner (0-6), but he has only had six runners to date. Do you give a top-class trainer the benefit of the doubt? Well I think we must. As I have previously stated, judge a trainer with a poor record after ten runners.

Another factor to consider also is the trainer's recent form. Luca Cumani is on the Trainers Hot List which is found in the Signpost section of the *Racing Post*. His second horse running at the course is a smartly bred two-year-old ridden by Ryan Moore (top jockey at the track). The horse cost 240,000gns, by far the most expensive purchase in the field. I know from experience that Luca Cumani is not a trainer who is normally associated with having two-year-olds ready to win first time out, but he does fire one in now and again and at the price quoted (16-1 SP with most of the mainstream bookies and 24.0 on Betfair early doors), surely this horse is worth a bet? The horse was called White Lake and won at a Betfair SP price of 40.0 (drifted massively from the 24.0 but we back to SP so these big drifts are in our favour). Another pleasing thing about taking a bit of a chance is that I also tipped this to my site members.

Goodwood (Flat Turf)

We have one qualifying trainer Roger Charlton (1).

His only runner on the card is running in a three-year-old handicap and has been penalised 2lbs for a previous win (82 up to 84) which means it qualifies for a bet on profile but did not qualify on price.

Saturday, August 23

Today we have meetings at Goodwood, Cartmel, Windsor, Redcar, Newmarket and York.

Goodwood (Flat Turf)

We have one qualifying trainer Roger Charlton (2). His first runner on the card is running in a Group 2 contest but does not qualify on price. His second runner is running in a handicap for the first time and qualifies on price.

Cartmel (National Hunt)

We have one qualifying trainer Donald McCain (3). His first two runners do not qualify on price, both quoted short-priced favourites. His third runner is first time in a handicap hurdle so qualifies for selection being unexposed and it also qualifies on price.

Windsor (Flat Turf)

We have three qualifying trainers Roger Varian (2), Andrew Balding (2) and Saeed Bin Suroor (1).

Roger Varian's first runner on the card does not qualify on price. His second is running in a Listed race off an unchanged Official Rating of 102 and is unexposed, so qualifies.

Andrew Balding's first runner qualifies as it is first time in a handicap. His second runner does not qualify on price.

Saeed Bin Suroor's only runner does not qualify on price.

Redcar

We have no qualifying trainers.

Newmarket

We have no qualifying trainers.

York

We have two qualifying trainers William Haggas (4) and Luca Cumani (3).

William Haggas's first runner is in a Group 3 but does not qualify as the horse has been raised from 102 to 114 (plus 12). His second runner has been raised 3lbs for winning a previous handicap (from 94 to 97), so qualifies as a bet. The horse is only a four-year-old and has only run six times so is still unexposed, it also qualifies on price. The third runner on the card is running in a handicap with its unchanged initial rating of 96 and qualifies on price. His last runner of the meeting runs in a handicap from an unchanged initial mark of 92 and qualifies on price. Both are fairly unexposed.

Luca Cumani's first runner on the card is running in a handicap but does not qualify having been raised from 89-99 (plus ten). His second runner is first time in a handicap and has only run three times so is totally unexposed. His last runner on the card again runs in a handicap but has been raised from 82-95 (plus 13), so does not qualify.

Sunday, August 24

Today we have meetings at Beverley, Goodwood and Yarmouth.

Beverley (Flat Turf)

We have one qualifying trainer, Mark Johnston (3). His first runner is in a maiden and has run twice (unexposed) so qualifies for selection. His second runner is in a three-year-old handicap and is still running from its initial mark of 79. The horse has had 14 starts so is looking exposed but ran well from this mark on its penultimate start. His last runner on the card is also in a three-year-old handicap and is only a 1lb higher than its last win 66-67 (plus 1lb). Again here I had to do some hard thinking about whether to back this horse or not as its profile is now looking totally exposed.

Goodwood

No qualifying trainers.

Yarmouth (Flat Turf)

We have three qualifying trainers William Haggas (2), Luca Cumani (1) and Philip McBride (1).

William Haggas's first runner did not qualify on price. His second runner is in an all-aged handicap running from its initial unchanged mark of 88. The horse has only run twice so is unexposed and qualifies on price.

Both the Philip McBride and Luca Cumani horses did not qualify on price.

Selections and results for the week

Points profit to date

24/8	Water Thief, King Of Macedon, Right Of Appeal, **Prince's Trust W9.99**	**1097.88**
23/8	Sir Walter Scott, Dare To Achieve, **Queensbury RulesW10.5**, Royal Mezyan Katchapoly, Hooded, Lizzie Tudor, Cameron Highland	**1092.34**
22/8	Semeen, Satellite, Ertijaal, Foreign Diplomat, **White LakeW40.0**, Perfect Pursuasion Indian Champ, Soul Instinct, **Swivel W 6.45**,	**1090.09**
21/8	**MubtaghaaW12.42**, Valley Of Fire, **Queen Of IceW27.0**, Sweet Charlie	**1056.86**
20/8	Mukhadram, Roossey, Stopped Out, Entihaa, Rocky Two, *Prince Of Islay, Gay Marriage, *Up Hill Battles, *Moonlight Venture, Incredible Fresh, Invasor Luck, Furos	**1021.41**
19/8	*Mambo Rhythm, Patronella, *Picture Postcard	**1037.41**
18/8	**Wahgah W8.8**, *Romance Story, Keeper's Ring	**1045.41**
		1043.00

As you can see from the table above our bank at the start of the week was 1043.00 points profit to date. Our bank increased by +54.88 points to 1097.88. I am not going to into any great detail analysing the week's results as I plan to do this for the whole of my results at the end of the book. But as you can see it has been a bit of a rollercoaster. From our 44 qualifying runners we found just seven winners, but it is the price of the winners that make this method so appealing and immensely profitable. We had a losing run of 17 which is scary, but I know the winners are coming and normally at good prices and I am prepared for this scenario as I have a bank to cover these losses.

The method may not appeal to most punters as it may not be selective enough and I agree to some extent on this point. But when you consider that there were 33 meetings in the week with a total of 2,219 runners declared to run, as a punter you have to look for a method that dramatically cuts down the horses you focus on or you have no chance of winning. I know we still had our fair share of runners, but the bottom line is that we made a tremendous profit on the week.

Summary of selection method

I am going to run over what I have written about above regarding finding selections and hopefully reconfirm and add some relevant points. You really do need to get the rules clear in your minds before you start to use the method. I am sure you must be getting to grips with the basics from the text so far. The information we require for the method is found in the pages of the *Racing Post*. To my knowledge I do not know of any other source that gives such detailed information about trainers' records at the tracks in this format.

Our first point is to find the race cards and the top trainers table at the meeting. Underline any trainer who has a minimum 20 per cent strike rate and shows a profit to a £1 level stake. Each trainer has a number after their name which denotes how many runners they have at the meeting. If a trainer has three runners, go to the race card and circle each runner as you come across them so you know that you have all of their runners on the day covered, missing any of their runners could be costly.

On the subject of the runners, note the trainer's overall strike rate at the course, initially this is his or her qualifying figure. Then look at a breakdown of the statistics in each of the categories: Flat racing — two-year-olds and three-year-olds; jumps — hurdlers, chasers and NHF.

Note: A trainer may have an excellent strike rate with his or her two-year-old runners at a track but an abysmal record with the three-year-old runners. Remember to check this, as with trainers over the jumps, hurdles, chasers and National Hunt Flat. Generally you will find that a trainer with the required strike rate of 20 per cent and above achieves this across the board, but you must check each category for qualifiers.

Next we have to check the prices of all of the qualifying runners (I will show you two ways of doing this a little later in the process). But the calculation is as follows: If a trainer has a 20 per cent strike rate, we divide 100 by 20 per cent which gives us a figure of five. This is the price we are looking for if we are backing this particular trainer's runners at the course. Therefore 5/1 SP or 6.0 (5+1) to reflect the decimal odds is what we are looking for on Betfair. This is a ballpark figure. If a horse's true price was 5.9 decimal and we were looking for 6.0 or above, I think I would still be backing it if it fits our profile.

The mainstream bookmakers seem keen to get prices out early these days and attract punters with offers such as best odds guaranteed. Most races are priced up around 9am, some handicaps the evening before. Much later, more like midday, the Betfair market will be taking shape. The real money does not start flowing into the Betfair market until minutes before the start of the actual race. This is why these markets take longer to form as traders on this site can get their fingers burned offering odds that reflect early bookmakers' prices. Betting markets are fluid and prices change throughout the day. Taking an early morning price can be a big mistake as the horse may drift quite dramatically or vice versa, you may gain by taking an early price.

The method I am going to show you takes in both scenarios and uses both the early bookmakers' prices and Betfair markets. I advise the selections from this method on my website at around 10am-11am each morning, often before. I have discovered a way of looking at the early morning prices the bookmakers are offering at around 9.30am-10am and backing the qualifying selections on Betfair, using Betfair SP. The method seems to work quite well, and all of my published results have been found using this it.

This is the method I recommend if you cannot watch live up-to-the-minute markets on Betfair. If you have time to bet on every qualifying selection using live markets then that would be the obvious thing to do, however betting live also brings sentiment into play. Are you disciplined enough to take a bad run without chasing losses? This is always the worry using this method and betting live (for me anyway). If you have had five losers on the day and the last selection is about to run, would you lose your discipline and up your stake to recoup losses?

Once I have found my selections for the day and circled all possible qualifiers in my *Racing Post* and gone through the form, I then need to look at the prices of these possible selections and eliminate the ones below my value price as shown using my calculation. There is an online site called www.oddschecker.com where you will find all early morning prices from all of the established online and high street bookmakers. I like to use this site as most, if not all, of the bookmakers' prices are displayed and you can take an average of the prices on offer. Go to the site and click on Racing on the menu bar (see below).

FRIDAY'S RACING

Haydock	13:30	14:00	14:30	15:00	15:35	16:10	16:45	17:20
Newmarket	13:40	14:10	14:40	15:15	15:45	16:25	17:00	17:30
Worcester	13:50	14:20	14:50	15:25	16:00	16:35	17:10	
Downpatrick	14:05	14:35	15:05	15:40	16:15	16:50	17:25	
Dundalk	17:40	18:10	18:40	19:10	19:40	20:10	20:40	21:10
Wolverhampton	17:45	18:20	18:50	19:20	19:50	20:20	20:50	21:20

Here is an example of how this works. In the 2.00 race at Haydock, we have two trainers with runners that fit our criteria of 20 per cent and above strike rate with runners who show a profit to £1 level stakes, Tom Dascombe and John Gosden. Click on the race to check out the early prices.

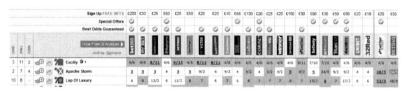

As you can see Excilly is odds-on favourite so can be immediately overlooked (Dascombe's runner). But Lap Of Luxury is quoted up to 15/2 to win the race. Gosden's strike rate is 29 per cent at the course, so we are looking for a price of 100 divided by 29 which equals 3.44 or above, 4.44 decimal. If you were to convert 15/2 into decimal you are looking at a price of 15 divided by two equals 7.5, so 8.5 decimal. This is way above the price considered to be value as we are beating our calculated odds for this runner, so at this stage it could be a bet.

The horse is quoted 11.0 on the Betfair site which is even bigger. John Gosden's runner fits our profile too as it is a two-year-old first time on the track, so is totally unexposed. Now we can definitely make this a selection as it fits all of our criteria. We have our first bet of the day. All of our bets are placed to Betfair SP and left to run using this method of staking. See below for how we place the bet on the Betfair site.

Click on the SP box (note all boxes in blue are to back a selection), the pink boxes adjacent to the blue are to lay a selection. Stay out of the pink!

Place your stake in the box, then click on Place bets box, job done. Just before the race is off you will be matched at the odds-on offer to Betfair SP. We don't know what the odds will be until the race is off, but I know that 99.9 per cent of the time I will beat the odds-on offer from the mainstream bookmakers and have never not been matched on a bet using this method.

Results and returns using Betfair:

◄ **14:00** ► **Haydock Park**

⬇ PDF Meeting Card

Irish Stallion Farms Ebf Vale Uk Maiden Fillies' Stakes (5) (D.I)

Going: Good (Good to Soft in places) | Distance: 6f | Age: 2yo | Total prize money: £4500 | Runners: 11 | Race Type: Flat

FULL RESULT

Pos (Draw)	Dist	Horse	Age	Wgt (OR)	Eq	Jockey Trainer	In-play High/Low	BSP/ISP (+/-)	Place
1 (6)		Lap Of Luxury	2	8-10	-	Robert Havlin John Gosden	50 / -	14.5 / 11 (28%)	2.87
2 (11)	½	Excilly	2	9	-	Richard Kingscote Tom Dascombe	- / 1.01	1.6 / 1.57 (0%)	1.09

Results and returns to SP:

Pos	Dist	Horse	Trainer	Age	Weight	Jockey	SP
1st (6)		10 Lap Of Luxury (IRE)	J H M Gosden	2	8-10	R Havlin	10/1
		SP 10/1 Raced centre, chased leaders, effort when edged right over 1f out, ran on to lead inside final furlong, ridden out opened 12/1					
2nd (11)	¼	3 Excilly	Tom Dascombe	2	9-0	R Kingscote	4/7f
		SP 4/7f Led stands side group and overall leader, hard ridden over 1f out, headed inside final furlong, kept on opened 4/6 £800-£1100 £400-£600					

You can see from the returns above how the Betfair SP compared to industry SP (the price offered by the mainstream bookies) and that it provided us with a big advantage, 14.5 compared to 10/1. We do have to pay commission on the bet and we have to deduct a point as the price is quoted as a decimal — 13.5 less five per cent commission of 0.67 leaving us with a profit of 12.83 — so we are in pocket by plus 2.83 using Betfair SP compared to industry prices. This is massive in the course of a year. The points gained actually start to pay for your losing bets (if you were to back to ISP). I have not had a bet that was not matched on Betfair. Also there is no one on the other end of a phone telling me I can't have a £100 bet on the selection as they will only allow me to have £40, which has happened to me quite a lot using both high street and online bookmakers.

BETFAIR AND BETTING EXCHANGES

Everyone should have at least one betting exchange account, but it seems that some people find it easier to bet with a traditional bookie. The concept of back and lay betting is alien to some, but it needn't be, and as I'll explain it really is quite simple. This is intended as a beginners' guide.

How do betting exchange odds work?

Betting exchanges are basically the middlemen in matching opposing views. If, say, you want to back a horse and your friend wants to lay it, you can organise a bet between you in the pub, after agreeing on the price, and amount. A betting exchange is similar except you won't know who you're betting with, and it doesn't have to be the same person who takes all of the other side of your bet. If your friend only wants to lay the horse to lose £20, then you can't get any more on. Not so on a betting exchange, your friend can still lay the horse to lose £20, but you can back it to win £1000 if you wish.

What is a matched bet?

Your bet is only on when it is 'matched'. This means that someone has taken the opposite side of the bet. The market will move constantly and in effect you are haggling for a price, the same as you might when buying a car. The deal is only done when both parties come to an agreement. On a betting exchange the deal is done, when the price someone is willing to lay at, is the same as the price someone is willing to back at.

Commission – you pay the betting exchange sites for acting as the middlemen

The betting exchanges will take a commission on your winnings for acting as the middlemen, and this will generally range from five per cent down to about one per cent, depending on the exchange, and the amount of commission you have paid previously. On Betfair the base rate is five per cent but that can be reduced to as low as two per cent. You would need to be a heavy user to get that low. Betfair also have a controversial premium charge for very successful users, but most won't have to worry about that, as you need to win quite a bit of money before it comes into effect.

Alternative ways of backing selections to squeeze the best prices out of the high street bookmakers could be to use the Tote. Most bookmakers will offer you this service as an alternative to SP. I have to say at this point that I don't think the Tote returns are as generous as they used to be since Betfred bought the chain, but it is still possible to beat SP, if we look at the example below.

2:00 - Irish Stallion Farms EBF
Vale UK Maiden Fillies' Stakes
(Bobis Race) (Div I)

» Full result

6f, Class 5, £2,911.05

1 Lap Of Luxury 10/1
2 Excilly 4/7F
3 Liberal Angel 25/1

NR: Twinkle Twinkle

10 ran Distances: ½l, 6l, 2l
TIME 1m 15.15s (slow by 4.15s)

Jockey: Robert Havlin
Trainer: John Gosden

WIN £12.00 PL £3.00, £1.10, £4.70

The Tote paid 12.00 which returns you 11/1 as opposed to 10/1 by the bookies and no commission to pay on this bet.

Merits of using Betfair

To increase my returns from the method, I back all of the selections with Betfair and all are backed to Betfair SP (BFSP), as I have already stated. Betfair is the biggest betting exchange on the internet and here we can find greater value than either the high street or online traditional bookmakers. In fact if you really want to maximise your profits using this method Betfair and Betfair SP are a must. I don't want to bore you explaining how the site works as I am sure now most of the betting population use this site. For a full explanation of how the site works go to www.betfair.com. Let me give you a few examples of why I use this site. Betfair SP usually beats the industry SP and because we are backing horses to win a race which are generally not considered a lot of the time by the press or the racing public, then from time to time we are going to hit some high-priced winners, this being the case then we can expect much greater returns using Betfair SP. Below are some examples:

2/7/2013 —	Overstep BFSP 36.0 ISP 25/1 +10
3/7/2013 —	Dantes King BFSP 38.0 ISP 20/1 +17
	Seal Of Approval BFSP 16.43 ISP 14/1 +1.43
	Bailey Storm BFSP 18.1 ISP 12/1 +5.1
	Divine Folly BFSP 19.28 ISP 11/1 +7.28

Taking a sample of just the five selections above would have made a huge difference to the bank with BFSP totals plus 127.81, industry SP totals plus 82 — a difference of 45.81 points. The way I look at this is Betfair SP is terrific value and it is very rare the industry returns match or beat them.

My other reason to use BFSP is that not only am I getting enhanced returns but the extra profit going into the bank pays for the losers we encounter. Betfair also beats Tote returns by quite a margin too and using BFSP eliminates chasing around different bookmakers searching for the best possible prices. Do I take the 25/1? Will it drift? Will it shorten up? Simply place the bets each day after finding your selections and get on with the rest of your day.

If you do have internet connection but don't want to use Betfair, then consider a best-odds guaranteed bookmaker. This way you can take early prices and if they drift throughout the day you get the higher price, a win- win situation. Of course the most accurate way of betting on the selections is to work out the odds we are looking for on the runners for each day and sit by your computer before each race is about to take place. The downside of this is that our first runner may be at 12.30pm in the National Hunt season and the last at 9.15pm if there is an evening meeting at Kempton on the same day. Also watching selections run may bring your emotions into play and if you have had a bad day (there will be plenty of these) you may start to chase losses.

I really do find that placing bets when the markets have formed and backing everything to Betfair SP is the best way forward. You can still watch live racing but the temptation to place further bets should not be an issue. This moves me on nicely to probably the second most important part of this strategy.

THE BACKER'S MINDSET

It is not only horse racing and greyhound racing that the high street bookmakers now cover, when you walk through the door it is hard to keep track of all of the action going on. Horse racing from Britain, Ireland, France, South Africa, and the USA, greyhound racing, virtual horse and dog racing, motor car racing, snooker, football, rugby and so it goes on. The biggest money spinners of all now are the casino machines which blurt out stupid noises that interrupt racing commentaries. You may have gathered that I am not a fan of high street shops anymore. If you have a weak constitution then it would not take you long to walk out of the door with empty pockets. The biggest gap without action I counted the last time I paid a visit to a high street shop was two minutes.

I don't want to sit and lecture anyone on how they should spend their money and if you have managed to become an expert in any or all of the above forms of sports and gaming, then good luck to you. I get a buzz out of backing a winner just like anyone else and to be honest, it was probably the initial buzz when I backed my first winner that drew me to the sport of horse racing in the first place, the lure of possible easy money. However I have learned some hard lessons along the way and also learned you must specialise in certain areas of your chosen sport and show extreme discipline to succeed.

When I devised this method and started to implement it myself and share it with subscribers to my site, many of my members despaired when I said I was going to publish the method in book form, as many think it will kill the prices if too many people use this method. Well at this moment in time I don't know whether this will be the case or not. But I am confident that many people will buy the method, lured in by the fantastic advertised profits, but it is how the profits are achieved that will sort out who has the discipline to succeed and who has not.

Making money from this method should be quite a simple task if you put the required bank to one side and start using the method by sticking to the rules rigidly. You know that in the long-term you are going to make money because we are backing horses at larger prices than the statistics state they should be. But of course along the way we are going to have a rocky ride with tremendous highs that are accompanied with the dreaded long losing runs.

If a long losing run was to happen during the first week you chose to try the method and put your money down, and just say you were faced with the longest losing run encountered to date (which is always a possibility), many of the people who have bought the book will consign it to the bin. They will think it is total rubbish, that the results published are fabricated and that I am the biggest con man ever to walk the face of the earth. But this is always a possibility with betting, horseracing in particular, nothing can be taken for granted. This is why we need a fairly secure bank which contains funds that are purely for the use of gambling, and if these funds are lost it will not affect your life in any way, shape or form. The money in the bank must have no emotional attachments.

The professional bettor's mindset

When placing a bet I prefer to stick with what I know or think I know something about. I have followed the sport of horse racing for the past 50 years. If I had not learned a thing or two in this time then I think I would be residing in the poor house by now. British horse racing in particular gives me a bit of a chance of beating the bookies at their own game. It may seem to be a bit of an unfair playing field as the book is always calculated in their favour, but I like to pit my knowledge and experience against the bookie and consider it a fair challenge regardless of the one-sided book. And it's a challenge that I am up for as I only have to back horses that I fancy and only ones I consider to be value. If my methods don't produce a bet on any particular day, I don't try to force one just for the sake of having a bet.

Horse racing has so many fixtures these days and it is difficult to keep track of all aspects of the sport. The winning mentality or mindset of the horse betting professional is one of the hardest things to adopt, day in and day out, but it is critical if you are to achieve any level of success and, more importantly, make a consistent income from your betting on horse racing or other mediums. I truly believe that this is the one thing that sets the top one per cent of elite betting professionals apart from the other 99 per cent of mug punters and gamblers who aspire to make money from their betting.

It is possible to teach people the skills required to become a successful bettor, how to set up their betting bank, how to set their stakes, how to read form and make selections. All this can be learned. However, each one of us naturally has different levels of risk we are willing to take, a different level of loss we are comfortable with, different levels of patience and of course discipline to stick to our rules. We are all naturally different in our character and this makes up what I call our 'mindset'.

We can all learn the same skills but each of us will apply them slightly differently. I know this from personal experience through the activity of subscribers to my website and through emails I receive on a daily basis. Many subscribers come and go, yet my information makes long-term profits. It is simply because they are not prepared to put the correct bank in place, stake my selections as advised, sit back and take the rough with the smooth and take a view to long-term profits. How simple is that? I can teach as many people as you like the same fundamental skills, even supply them all with the same daily selections and set them a level to start with their banks, yet each one will end up eventually with different totals in the bank. So how do we change our mindset? What is the mindset of the horse betting professional versus the punter?

The first thing we must do is look at the likely characteristics the horse betting professional has as his mindset.

Decisive — The first thing I always notice about the bettors who are successful, is how decisive they are in their betting. They make decisions and stick to them, whereas the average punter is unsure about things and constantly flitting from one system to the next, always changing his mind about the likely winner.

Patient — Professional bettors are also very patient and realise that they make profits month by month and season by season, not necessarily day by day or race by race. Most punters are quite the opposite, always trying to push things and chase their losses if they have a losing bet. They have a very short-term approach. I have a quote on my website 'get-rich-quick merchants not welcome'. Many of my mug punter friends have loads of money one day then are skint the next.

Emotionally Detached — By managing their money correctly the professionals do not worry about the outcome of each bet, but are quietly confident that month after month they will make money from the methods they apply. The punter who has little money management skills will always be worried about every bet. He will be staking more and more to try to make a profit and lose more and more chasing losses.

Disciplined — The professional always bets logically and rationally, each bet is well researched and will give him every chance of success. He knows that over time his selections will make him a profit. The punter will simply gamble making uninformed selections based on nothing more than irrational hunches or hearsay or on a gut feeling.

Bet within their means — Back to money management again. The pro always knows exactly what stake he is placing and why. He will always bet within the confines of his betting bank. The punter will be betting with money that is needed for other things, so becomes emotionally attached to it and the importance of the result.

Accepts Results With Equanimity — The professional bettor will not be the one jumping up and down at the side of the race track when his horse wins or cursing his luck if it loses but will leave that to the mug punters and gamblers who take everything personally. The professional knows tomorrow is another day and that the profits will come. He realises that in horse racing and betting your overall profits are what matter.

Now for a tip. Sit down for a few minutes and be honest with yourself — what are your strengths and what areas do you need to work on? You need to start forming the habits of success and create yourself a winning character when you bet. The person I have described above probably does not exist, as we all have our strengths and weaknesses and are all prone to making the odd error and mistake, that's what makes us human. But if you can take on board and adopt as many of the above attributes as possible then you are taking giant steps in the right direction. Photocopy this page, stick it on your computer monitor and refer to it on a daily basis.

Patience and Discipline — Above all else you must develop superb levels of patience and discipline to stick to your 'betting strategy'. This is so easy when you are on a winning streak and the profits are rolling into your betting bank, but what do you do when you are going through that long losing run? The run that lasts a week without a winning selection, when you know you have read the form and picked the best horse in the race and it still does not perform. This is when the true professional is disciplined and has faith in his strategy and ability. It is true that the longer you are involved in horse betting, the easier it gets, not just from what you learn, but more importantly because you have experienced the highs and the lows. You have had the good runs to see you through the bad runs. You know that you can weather the storm.

I am sure you are now beginning to realise that the life of a true horse racing betting professional is hard work day in day out, week after week. The professional is out there working hard, perfecting betting strategies and making slow, consistent profits. He will be building up his betting bank, increasing stakes and hopefully making a great income from his chosen sport, many days breaking even, many making a loss before the profits come in on the big days. Sometimes you may only have four to five of these days all month but these possibly bring in 90 per cent of your profits. However it is how you approach the remaining days that will set you apart as a winner or make you quit as another disillusioned punter who tried and failed. This is what sets the true professional apart from the remaining 99 per cent.

Hopefully the information in this book will help you considerably on your path to becoming a successful punter. I don't expect anyone to read this book then walk into their manager's office the following day and hand in their notice. There are many professional people making more money than myself from their chosen careers who have got there through sheer hard work and determination. I dread getting up some mornings just like the next person especially if I am on a losing run. I am not trying to promote the life of a professional gambler as the be all and end all, but betting can be fun, so let's try and make it as much fun as possible while also being profitable.

BANKING AND STAKING

I will never forget going to Wetherby races with a friend who had started his own business with money he had won from the bookies. I was going as the form student who would sort out the winners. In return I got to use one of his member's badges and enjoy a free lunch. On that day I learned a very valuable lesson. On the way there in the car after discussing the selections I had sorted out for us, he asked, 'How much have you brought with you to lose?' I had never given a thought to losing the money I had in my wallet, not because I didn't think that I would, but I suppose I treat each day's racing with a great deal of optimism and losing money never really came into my head, especially all of the money I was carrying with me.

However my friend firmly pointed out to me that if I was to win at this game, I had to separate money I was using for betting from any other source of funds, it had to be money I could afford and expect to lose. Looking back, this was possibly the best piece of advice offered to me by anyone to this day. By the way we cleaned up so no need to worry on this particular day. I have never been one to go mad after a win and splash out on something extravagant. This doesn't mean I haven't enjoyed the money when I have had a big win (there is no point betting if you cannot treat yourself when you have a winner or two), but I have always put some of my winnings to one side as I know there will be bad times around the corner.

If you research a strategy that may with luck make you long-term profits, you must take time out to analyse the results to see how you can best stake the method, to ensure you can get the maximum profit from the set of results you are examining. Your plan must get you over the inevitable losing runs, while protecting some of your likely profits which the method produces.

I look back on my early punting days in slight horror. My methods at the time were probably better than the ones I use now and were very solid indeed. I backed plenty of good-priced winners with a very high strike rate, but my approach to banking and staking was naive to say the least, basically non-existent. If I had taken a more professional approach and brought the whole package to the table, my sound selection method coupled with a bank and some kind of staking plan would have made me a very wealthy young man. My indiscipline reduced any realistic chance I had of making a living out of betting and scuppered my chance of making long-term, consistent profits. It wasn't my fault, I just didn't know any better at the time. It is only reading books by professional bettors and articles in papers that have honed my own skills and taught me the necessary discipline required to become successful.

I have learned through my past experiences that with every method I have developed, the correct bank and stakes to cover the inevitable losing runs must be in place. You can then move forward and hopefully go on to produce the long-term profits that your painstaking research deserves. If we fail in our initial preparation then we stand little chance of beating the bookies and making money from the game.

I actually started backing the selections from this method on July 1, 2013 after my initial research had shown this method had great potential. I know from past experience that a selection method that goes for longshots will have long losing runs and selections can usually only be backed to level stakes. I also know that many of the selections will be unplaced so each-way betting is also out of the question. Selections must be backed to win only.

I have recorded results that span 17 months. This is a very good sample to show how the method performs and is likely to perform in the future. As we know, what has happened in the past does not necessarily happen in the future and trying to predict future results is pure conjecture. However as I only follow trainers with a minimum 20 per cent and above strike rate at any given course from a big sample of their runners, then this is the strike of winners I expect to achieve in the long term. This figure is not constant, for instance that for every five runners I will have a winner (20 per cent), but I know from experience we are going to have relatively short winning runs and I know that long losing runs are inevitable. The big prices dictate this will happen and it does.

For whatever reason, winners seem to come in clusters as do the losers. As we are generally looking at horses around the 6.0 mark in the forecast betting, then unfortunately our losing runs will vastly outweigh our winning runs. Study the table below which shows the losing runs we are likely to encounter which helps point us to the size of the bank required.

Strike Rate (%)	Maximum Losing Run
95	2
90	3
85	4
80	4
75	5

Strike Rate (%)	Maximum Losing Run
70	6
65	7
60	8
55	9
50	10
45	12
40	14
35	16
30	19
25	24
20	**31**
15	43

Note that the above table is based on mathematical analysis. If you don't have a good sample of past results then the above table is very helpful in determining your bank size. We do however have a good sample of past results to aid us in determining the bank required.

From the above table we can see that with a strike rate of 20 per cent we are likely to encounter a longest losing run of around 31. This is the table I used to determine my initial bank. We also have to strike a balance of trying to eliminate the risk of totally losing the bank yet allowing the bank to grow. A large bank with small stakes is ideal but if the stakes are too low and the bank grows too slowly, this scenario would possibly make you lose interest in the method. Yet the opposite scenario, small banks large stakes would have you on the edge of your seat. Ideally medium, steady growth with limited risk is our aim. We know betting on horses is a very risky pastime and nothing is guaranteed, but if you are serious about making money from the game or having some fun bets, a sensible, calculated approach is required to give yourselves some chance of winning long term.

Let me just make a very important point here. As I have already discussed, any bank must be money that has no other use but to gamble with. It must be money you can afford to lose, and if lost will not affect any future plans you may have such as for holidays, mortgage repayments or bills. While the method has made very good profits to date and has been thoroughly researched, there are no future guarantees of success.

The table states that our longest losing run with a 20 per cent strike rate is 31. The method to date has a 20 per cent strike rate which is brilliant when you consider that we are looking at trainers with a minimum 20 per cent strike rate, but the prices of our winners easily exceed 5/1. Since we look at prices 5/1 or above then I expect the losing runs to be higher than 31. See the results tables which detail the longest losing sequence to date and biggest loss to the bank in points.

Now on to a very important part of my staking plan. If you remember earlier in the book I mentioned to note how many runners the trainer has at the course (figure after the trainer's name in the course trainers list). If the trainer has just one runner at the track I stake two points on this horse. This is going to have an effect on the size of our bank. Initially when thinking about betting to level stakes I was happy to sit on a 100-point bank, but after noting the significance of trainers sending just one runner to a course I decided to double up my stake on these runners. I revised my view on the bank size and used a 200-point bank, which would serve me better.

This is not an enormous bank when you consider the huge profits made to date and a bank that is comfortably above our losing run. We had a losing run of 39 but more significantly a loss to the bank of 74 points as some of these selections carried a double stake. At this point you may be thinking, well the 100-point bank would still be OK and yes it would, but it would be a little too close for comfort for me. I have a theory that once your bank looks under threat then panic can set in and you might just start to do silly things, such as chasing losses or not using the proven profitable method. I have learned that scared money never wins, and a surplus is good to have. Two hundred points should be the size of your bank, your initial bank size divided by 200 is the initial stake to use, and only put aside a bank you can afford.

Growing the bank

How to grow the bank? What a great dilemma to have. And as our bank grows when should I increase my stakes? This actually may not apply if your initial bank had sufficient funds and you are happy with the returns the method makes. This scenario would mean that any time profits are greater than the initial bank you take the money out and spend it. That is the end game for all who use this method and the perfect scenario. But I do believe that when using a method that is new, that also has long losing runs, you should start small to get a feel for the method and also get your mindset right. Is the method one you think you can employ successfully? If so, then aim to build up to a level where you can start taking profits and enjoy the fruits of your labour at some stage. I also believe the best way of doing this if starting small is to compound. Simply add the profit back to the bank until you reach a level where you can consider increasing your stakes and the end goal of taking money out to spend.

Now I actually believe we all have a level when we start to feel a little edgy when the size of the bets we are placing start to increase. We all have different levels of risk that we are prepared to take. Once this level is reached and the stakes you are placing make you feel a little uneasy then you are out of your comfort zone. It is at this level you must consider to start taking profits. Staking above your comfort zone will make you feel anxious and this is not fun. At this level it is likely you could start breaking all of the hard and fast rules you set yourself, start taking the profits and enjoy spending the bookies' money.

Compounding

From mighty oaks little acorns grow. Consider compounding. I honestly believe that this is the best way to stake any method that is new to you and a way of addressing your bank and staking. Once you have placed the initial amount of money you can afford to lose into your betting account, divide this bank by 200, this will be your initial stake and starting point. With good luck and tight money management skills you are now equipped with a bank that should see you ride the likely highs and lows the method produces. It is obviously fantastic to start off with a winning day, week or month. Most months have been profitable with the exception of two when a loss was made, strangely enough both November, the end of the Flat turf season and the start of the National Hunt proper.

Again I was offered some sound advice a long time ago by a fellow professional punter about compounding. He was using a method that I had developed that was doing extremely well at the time. Both of our banks were growing in unison and I had stated that once my bank had doubled then I would double my stake. The advice he gave me was as follows. If a selection method is doing well and you are making money from it then obviously your bank is going to grow. The reason for employing a bank is because there are risks attached, otherwise you would not need this bank in the first place. The bank is to try to get you over the expected losing runs. His advice was not to double stakes when the bank has doubled otherwise the risk level to your bank never diminishes. Rather than live with the risk, try to reduce it as the bank increases. His solution to this would be if a starting bank of say £200 doubled to £400 using £1 stakes, do not increase stakes to £2 at this time, but only increase to £1.50.

This way of compounding means that your bank has still increased, but you have added 50 per cent of your profit to your stakes and 50 per cent to your bank. You have still given the bank the chance to move forward, yet also reduced your level of risk, hence making it harder for the bookies or your adversaries on Betfair to get that money back, as long as you remain disciplined. Following this staking plan, hopefully you will eventually achieve the level of staking that brings you to your comfort zone and you can start taking profits. Sound advice and you can see why this ex-coal miner became a very successful punter.

WHEN NOT TO BET

Note: This method has not been used or tested for Irish racing results to date. All are from UK race courses.

There are not many conditions for not having a bet, but you must apply the following rules to increase profitability. Take a look at the runners below and I will highlight why this is a no-bet race.

1 ⁵ 4222	EVENING RAIN p ☑☐☑☐☒ 17	2	9-7 82	Kevin Stott 5 Saeed bin Suroor 74	—	89	9/2
2 ⁹ 11035	DITTANDER ☑☐☑☐☒ 47	2	9-4 79	Cam Hardie 3 Richard Hannon 47	80	90	40
3 ³ 431	KOPTOON t ☑☐☑☐☒ ⬛ 21	2	9-3 78	Richard Kingscote Tom Dascombe 45	75	91	2
4 ⁶ 101304	L'ETACQ ☑☐☑☐☒ ⬛⬛ 25	2	8-13 74	Richard Hughes Richard Hannon 47	43	90	10
5 ⁴ 2242	RUSSIAN HEROINE ☑☐☑☐☒ 9	2	8-10 71	Ryan Moore Sir Michael Stoute 71	—	92	9/2
6 ¹⁰ 010612	GOLD WALTZ ☑☐☑☐☒ ⬛⬛ 40	2	8-9 70	Pat Dobbs Ralph Beckett 60	90	90	11/2
7 ⁷ 165	L'ADDITION ☑☐☑☐☒ ⬛⬛⬛ 44	2	8-9 70	Ted Durcan William Jarvis 50	59	90	13/2
8 ¹ 336135	EMEF ROCK ☑☐☑☐☒ ⬛ 18	2	8-8 69	Martin Dwyer Mick Channon 38	—	89	22
9 ⁸ 345564	MYLAPORYOURS h1 ☑☐☑☐☒ 7	2	8-5 66	David Probert Rod Millman 50	56	83	66
10 ² 0370	YORKIE TALKIE ☑☐☑☐☒ 11	2	8-2 63	Joe Fanning Mark Johnston 44	—	91	20

Firstly, do not bet if any of the qualifying trainers have more than two runners entered in a particular race. Our qualifying trainers in this race are highlighted in blue. Out of the ten declared runners we have five covered. This is an impossible race to bet in and even if we did cover all five at the quoted odds, we are most likely to lose on the race if the shortest priced selection wins. Therefore it is better to leave such races alone. Stick with races where there are no more than two qualifiers from our selection method.

Also remember to take all qualifying trainers into consideration from the master list — any trainer who qualifies as having a minimum 20 per cent strike rate at a course and shows a level stakes profit. Ignore the other sections such as trainers' records with two-year-olds, three-year-olds, hurdlers, chasers and NHF. Take their overall record into account here.

On the same day, we have another no-bet situation that again rarely occurs these days which is horses running out of the handicap. In the Nottingham 4.20 race, we have a qualifying selection in Art Scholar. The horse has won off a mark of 93 in the past and but today has to run from a mark of 86, 5lbs higher than its Official Rating. This is flagged up at the bottom of the race in Long Handicap.

10²	ART SCHOLAR p	7	8-10	Oisin Murphy
646374	🏇▦◫☐✕ 🎴 21		76	Michael Appleby 63
11⁵	GREEN LIGHT	3	8-5	Hayley Turner
254028	🏇▦◫☐✕ 18		80	Ralph Beckett 60

Long Handicap: Art Scholar 8-5, Green Light 8-4

As you can see from the above screen shot today, Art Scholar is set to carry 8-10 but in the Long Handicap is set to carry 8-5 which means the horse has to pull a little bit more out of the bag to win today and is best left alone. This is also flagged up in the Spotlight section of the *Racing Post.*

Art Scholar: Dual C&D winner for whom conditions will be fine, but he´s not the force he once was and recent form suggests he´s up against it from 5lb out of the handicap.

Other times when I will not bet are at mixed meetings. These are quite common at Lingfield where they have mixed all weather and turf meetings in the summer. I also don't bet at mixed Flat and jumps meetings, again where the card is split between the two very different disciplines. The reason I don't bet is that when this happens it tends to mess with the statistics and therefore the normal trends for the particular meeting.

The above anomalies do not occur often but must be flagged up for your attention.

Odds-on favourites

Never be scared of backing against an odds-on favourite. Obviously when such a situation occurs our qualifiers are going to be a big price to beat the favourite and I have backed many a good-priced winner by taking on odds-on shots. However common sense must prevail and if you are looking at taking on something 1/3, 1/4, 1/5 or shorter in the betting, look for chinks in the favourite's profile (which are very likely none). If no negatives can be found then it is silly to back against these favourites just for the sake of it. I would certainly take on any newcomer at any odds simply because they are talking horses that are showing up well on the gallops but lack experience in a race.

For example, the prestigious Middle Park Stakes, a Group 1 race for two-year-old colts was being run at Newmarket on Friday, October 17, 2014. The hot odds-on favourite was Ivawood whose trainer Richard Hannon was a qualifier for us as he had a 20 per cent strike rate with his two-year-olds at the course, however the horse's odds were a restrictive 1-2 so it was obviously not a bet for us. But we had another qualifying trainer with a runner in the race, Charlie Appleby. His runner was quoted 12/1 in the early prices so qualified. All day I was thinking to myself that Appleby's horse had no chance of beating the favourite, but the method made it a bet so I had to go against my gut instinct. All of the tipsters went for the favourite and this was the *Racing Post's* verdict too.

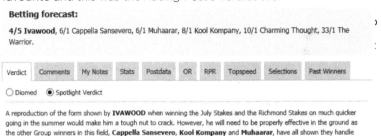

Betting forecast:

4/5 Ivawood, 6/1 Cappella Sansevero, 6/1 Muhaarar, 8/1 Kool Kompany, 10/1 Charming Thought, 33/1 The Warrior.

Sticking with the rules and ignoring my gut instinct paid off massively for me. Who am I to try to pretend that I knew Ivawood was a better horse than Charming Thought? Both lightly raced, progressive two-year-old colts. Remember it is the bookies who dictate the odds by sheer weight of money, generally from punters who have taken in all of the hype from the press. A horse at 1-2 in the betting is very, very poor value anyway. The verdict in the *Racing Post* stated the favourite had not encountered such soft ground conditions. This was the chink in its armour.

The price of selections

The biggest priced winner I have had to date is 50.0 which is quite amazing. I am very wary of backing selections above this price. I know there is a 100/1 shot lurking in the wings but if a selection is a massive price it is for a reason and I am wary of these selections and generally leave them alone.

Finally a word on the ground. If the going is quoted heavy then of course it's a concern, but I leave this to the trainer's discretion. If they have a 20 per cent and above strike rate at the course, I think they know better than me if the horse is capable of going on the ground.

Other factors

I have already touched on trainers sending just the one runner to a meeting and that I stake two points on their single runners. All other bets are one point stakes. Now I have been using this selection method for a while, I am getting a feel for the trainers and runners at particular tracks and the results I have recorded to date are using 1-2 point stakes. You must stick with this method of staking initially and I advocate that you do. But there is some useful additional information printed in the *Racing Post* which I suggest you take time to look at on a daily basis. This additional information may just improve your profits if you take note of some of these other factors.

Once I have my qualifiers marked off for the day and my stakes sorted out, I take time to browse the Signpost section of the paper. You may just strengthen the case of many of the selections, and as I have stated initially I do not advocate you sway from my simple staking plan. You may, when you get a feel for using this additional information, see something that stands out when taking in these additional factors.

In the Signpost section there are lots of different categories listed, the ones I note are as follows:

Jockey Bookings — Obviously a good jockey riding our selection who has a good strike rate for the trainer is a positive. If it's one of the top jockeys riding, Ryan Moore or Richard Hughes for example, then that is a massive positive. The downside for us is that the price will reflect this, but there are many other good jockeys who trainers are keen to book.

Claiming Jockeys — Do not be put off if a claiming jockey is riding for our trainer. Remember that we are backing trainers with a terrific strike

rate at the course and his judgement is obviously very good.
Top stables will book good claiming jockeys if they think their horse is high enough in the handicap. Do not take claiming jockeys allowances into account when looking at the horses' ratings in handicaps. The jockeys need this allowance in most cases to give them a chance against the more experienced riders, but some claimers are better than some seasoned jockeys even with their claim. Natural ability is the phrase I am searching for.

Course Specialists — Another handy reference to trainers who seem to target this particular meeting and race with their mounts.

Race Trace — Same as above but when specific races are targeted.

Handicap Debut and First Time Blinkers — Both these sections are of interest to me. If the trainer has a 20 per cent or above strike rate with their handicap debutants they could have got into the race under the radar. The same with the use of blinkers, these may just bring a little improvement to the horse's form to date. But again make sure the 20 per cent is achieved from a good sample of runners. I normally look at no less than three winners to date. If any of my shortlisted horses appear on any of the above lists in the Signpost sections, I may be tempted to up my stakes slightly. Also if I get a really good feel about a horse that appears in some of the lists above, I will have the odd strong bet, especially if it is the trainer's only runner at the track. Believe me I have landed a few strong bets at big odds. As I have already mentioned, don't let the price of the horse put you off.

Hot Trainers — If a trainer is in blistering form then this is when the bulk of the winners are coming from his or her stable. It is fascinating to see how one month a trainer can be sending winners in all over the place, then all of a sudden they tend to dry up. Note again here, do not detract from the method rules because the trainer is not on the hot list. These are additional pointers to the bets you have already marked off. The RFT section of the Signpost section is also of interest when it comes to pointing out trainers in form.

A perfect example

On July 2, 2014 I had marked off my qualifiers for the day and had come across seven. Once I have marked off my bets and noted whether they are one or two point bets, I tend to have a browse through the *Racing Post* to see if any of the bets have outstanding claims (do not be influenced by any tipsters' comments). One horse in particular that stood out to me on the day was a horse trained by Ian Williams. Now he is a trainer I like a lot. I have noted many times that when the money is down for any of his runners they win or go very close. This proves the man knows his job, but he also seems to fire in the odd big-priced winner, so is also capable of getting one or two ready that go under the radar, and this day I thought I had discovered one.

The horse in question was Almanak. I had already placed my asterisk at the side of the horse when going through the selections (my signal to have two points on this particular selection) as it was the trainer's only runner at the course. But as I have stated, when you have your runners for the day have a good look at their credentials, and by this I mean are there any other hard facts that seem to give this particular runner a strong chance on paper.

Ian Willams at the time was on the Hot Trainers List. His horses had been running up to their mark recently, highlighted in the RFT section. The horse was flagged up in the Course Specialist section and also Nathan Alison the jockey was highlighted in the Jockey Bookings section. All in all this horse looked to have a heck of a lot going for it on the day. I took a little more time to look through the horse's lifetime form history and noted that the horse had been brought over from Ireland. It had been rated as high as 92 over there but today was racing off 67 (see below).

	Date	Course	Wt	Result	Jockey	OR		
▶	02Jul14	Kem 6St C5Hc 2K	9-2	1/10 (shd Lucky Di 8-10) 16/1	Nathan Alison	67	*	*
▶	06Jun14	Cat 6Sft C6Hc 2K	9-7	11/12 (11L Cadeaux Pearl 9-2) p 14/1	Shane Gray	65	*	*
▶	12Apr14	Thi 7GS C5Hc 2K	9-2	11/16 (17½L Flexible Flyer 9-4) tp 20/1	George Downing	69	*	*
▶	21Mar14	Wol 5St C4Hc 5K	8-13	7/7 (11L Muhdiq 9-5) 14/1	George Downing	79	*	*
▶	13Nov13	Dun 7St Hc 5K	9-9	7/8 (7¼L Rummaging 9-4) t 12/1	Billy Lee	83	*	*
▶	01Nov13	Dun 6St Hc 10K	9-3	8/10 (6¼L English Deer 9-5) t 20/1	Wayne Lordan	88	*	*
▶	27Jun13	Tip 5GF 3yHc 5K	9-5	7/7 (6L Johnny Lynch 9-5) tp 7/1	Shane Gray	85	*	*
▶	06Jun13	Tip 5GF Hc 7K	9-2	8/12 (6L Abstraction 8-13) t 10/1	Wayne Lordan	89	*	*
▶	10May13	Chs 5GS C23yHc 15K	8-7	9/10 (7¾L Normal Equilibrium 8-9) t 20/1	Shane Gray	90	*	*
▶	28Sep12	Dun 5St 2yHc 16K	9-2	2/9 (shd All Ablaze 8-4) t 8/1	Wayne Lordan	90	*	*
▶	25Aug12	Cur 5Hy 2yL 21K	9-3	7/7 (17½L Three Sea Captains 9-3) t 20/1	Billy Lee	92	*	*
▶	30Jun12	Cur 6Sft/Hy 2yG2 47K	9-3	6/6 (10½L Probably 9-3) t 14/1	Wayne Lordan	—	*	*
▶	18May12	Dun 5St 2y 5K	9-5	1/5 (1¾L Truly Madly 9-0) t 4/5F	Wayne Lordan	—	*	*
▶	04May12	Dun 5St 2y 7K	9-5	3/8 (2L Tennessee Wildcat 9-5) 11/4J	Wayne Lordan	—	*	*

I was obviously concerned that since the horse had run in this country it hadn't really shown much form, but a little bit of money for the horse early doors (highlighted on the www.oddschecker.com site under market movers) was enough to make my mind up to have a decent bet on it that day as it had so many positive factors going for it. Regardless of any of the above additional information, the system had made it a two point bet anyway. The horse got up to win by a short head. Apart from nearly giving me a heart attack watching the race, I had one of my biggest wins at 24.39 on Betfair. Just for good measure I had backed him in the town with three of the high street bookies at SP which was 16/1. That little bit of extra study paid off, and this is not a one-off for me. Take time to look and get a feel for the Signpost section of the *Racing Post*. It could pay off somewhere down the line.

I have a cautionary note here too. Do not overthink a horse's chances of winning or losing. The above was a bet for me regardless of any of the additional information, and let me also state here while I am on the subject, that any time I have ever thought of not backing a selection is when I have read comments about the horse's chances in the papers. If a horse is a selection back it at all costs. If a horse is a 40/1 shot in the betting then of course it will get negative comments from the press, but it must remain a selection regardless of this. Have a good look through the results

From this method, remember my biggest winner to date is 50.0.

Support

Although I think that I have covered every angle regarding finding the selections, I am pretty sure someone will have a question or questions to ask about some aspect of the method. I give ongoing support to anyone who has purchased the book for as long as it takes to grasp the method. Sometimes it can be a simple matter that is causing the reader a problem and can be resolved quite quickly by sending me an email at the following address tonybettingsystem@gmail.com.

You can also go to my website www.bettingsystem.info where I offer one-to-one tuition on how to get selections by going through one week of *Racing Post's* demonstrating how I arrived at these in that week and my selections for the day's racing. Tuition is also included on my other strategies I may be using at the time that are making me a profit.

QUICK FIRE SUMMARY

- Go to the *Racing Post's* Race Cards.
- Go to the Top Trainers List.
- Mark off all trainers who have a minimum 20 per cent strike rate at the course who show a level stakes profit to a £1 stake.
- Trainers must have had at least ten winners at the track.
- Check the betting to make sure the possible selection qualifies on price which must equal or beat the trainer's strike rate at the course. For example, trainer has a 20 per cent strike rate (100 divided by 20 equals five) so the price of the horse must be 5/1 (6.0 decimal) or above.
- Check the different categories to see if the trainer maintains a 20 per cent and above strike rate across the board — Flat two-year-olds and three-year-olds, National Hunt hurdlers, chasers and National Hunt Flat (trainer must have had ten winners).
- Ignore horses that do not qualify from any of the above categories, but give trainers the benefit of the doubt if only a small sample of runners (less than ten).
- Check to see if the horse has an unexposed/exposed profile (generally unexposed running in non-handicap races). If handicaps and penalised for a win, must be no higher 5lbs.
- Check for penalised novices if penalised more than 5lbs for a win.

Do not bet if:

- There are three qualifying trainers or more with runners in the same race.
- If the horse is out of the handicap.
- The horse's price exceeds 50.0.
- Horses have been penalised more than 5lbs.

All selections backed to Betfair SP if possible.

Note: All selection methods have losing runs and some exceed our expectations. Make sure you have the correct bank in place to cover these losses.

MONTHLY BREAKDOWN OF RESULTS TO DATE

Month	Selections	Winners	Losers	Strike Rate	Profit
July 2013	95	32	63	34%	**+249.57**
August	109	30	79	30%	**+168.50**
September	64	12	52	19%	**+83.22**
October	61	15	46	26%	**+38.25**
November	106	18	88	17%	-4.81
December	105	19	86	18%	**+27.38**
January 2014	66	13	53	20%	**+54.09**
February	67	13	54	19%	**+52.53**
March	73	13	60	18%	**+6.33**
April	94	14	80	15%	**+21.65**
May	110	33	77	30%	**+126.81**
June	113	28	85	25%	**+37.96**
July	145	30	115	21%	**+192.27**
August	144	22	122	15%	**+29.14**
September	142	17	125	12%	**+36.39**
October	125	21	104	17%	**+169.68**
November	107	8	99	7%	-45.39
December	69	11	58	16%	**+110.77**
TOTALS	1795	349	1446	19.44	**1316.66**

RETURN ON INVESTMENT TO DATE = **Points Staked 2329, Profit 1317 = 56%**
LONGEST LOSING RUN TO DATE = **39**
LONGEST LOSING RUN FOR POINTS LOST = **73.62**

A quick review of the results: Note that the only two losing months have both been in November. This·month heralds the start of the National Hunt season and the end of the Flat turf season. Generally this is not an easy time for punters and it may be just a coincidence, but worth noting if another November returned a loss.

FULL DETAILED
RESULTS TO DATE

DATE	WINNERS / LOSERS	TOTAL BFSP
30/12	*Lackaday, W14.0,*Salmon Sushi W6.2, *Millionaires Row, Amella, *Perfect Rhythm , Amanto, Lumpys Gold	1316.66
28/12	Haaf A Sixpence,*Pennys Double	1289.08
27/12	Grandouet , Woodland Walk, Albert Bridge,*Belle De Londres, *Scrafton, Sinndar's Man, Captain Koko	1292.08
22/12	Ovilia, *Shyron,*Keepers Ring	1301.08
20/12	*AnglophileW4.9, Ulbatique	1306.08
19/12	Significant Move,*Rita's Boy	1299.67
18/12	*Danseur Noble, *Activation, Premier Portrait,Tiger Feat, *Wild At Midnight	1302.67
16/12	*Artistic Queen	1297.36
15/12	*Little Lord Nelson	1299.36
14/12	Bay Wing	1301.36
13/12	*Uganda Glory W38.0	1302.36
12/12	Cardinal Walter W7.48, Hassle, Dreams Of Milan	1232.06
10/12	Until Winning, Henri De Boistron, *Barracuda Boy, *Gold Flash W6.2, *Stay Strong	1227.90
9/12	Abigail Lynch W11.0, Cogry, Bameitalonmyroots	1224.02
8/12	Oscatara, Desoto County, New Style, Beta Tauri, Foxtrot Jubilee	1216.52
7/12	Mrs Peachey, Robins Reef, DioclesW11.41	1221.52
6/12	Caracci Apache W21.41, Snake EyesW4.48, Sweet Deal, Oscar Whiskey	1213.63
5/12	*Dianora, *Lysander The Greek	1191.98
4/12	Green Tornado	1195.98
3/12	Perfect Orange, Ballista, Madrasa, BalmusetteW3.21, Ballyfarsoon, Ioannou	1196.98
2/12	The Dream Fast,Tidal Way	1199.89
1/12	Where'd Ya Hide It, Sperrin, *Ambella	1201.89
29/11	Haaf A Sixpence, Energia Flavio, Cerutty, Front Run, *Rock Charm	1205.89
28/11	Style Setter,Red Spinner, *Artistic Queen,*Lacan	1210.89
27/11	LogorrheicW9.36, Foxtrot Jubilee	1216.89
26/11	*Matraash, *Thomas Blossom, *Greenlaw, *Hallelujah	1209.95
25/11	*Miami Gator,Laughing Rock	1217.95
24/11	Lough Kent, TheinvalW5.65	1220.95
22/11	*Super Kid,*Genax ,*Viva Verglas,*Estikhraaj	1217.53
21/11	Dans Wee Man,*Lola Montez, *Ghazi	1221.53
20/11	*Knight Owl,*Ambella	1226.53
19/11	*Thames Knight,*Salmon Sushi, *Jacueline Jouliac, *Foxford, Sublimation, Zipp	1230.53

DATE	WINNERS / LOSERS	TOTAL BFSP
18/11	Greenhead High, Lewisham, Carron Valley,*Activation, Argaki, *I'm Super Too	1240.53
17/11	*Fred Le Macon	1248.53
15/11	Yorkist *Pure Line, Stellar Jet, Sylvette	1250.53
14/11	Carrigeen Lantana,*Heho DH 12.5, *Almanack, *Stilla Afton , *London Mayor, Sbraase	1255.53
13/11	*Logorrheic,*Prying, Ace Marmalade, Senor George, Miami Gator	1253.60
12/11	Across The Bay, Vital Evidence, Sindarban	1260.60
11/11	Hi George, My Wigwam Or Yours	1263.60
10/11	True Course, Shady McCoy, Pathway To Honour, Conroy, PacifyW42.0, Poyle Toby *Net Work Rouge	1265.60
9/11	*Strumble Head, Dan's Wee Man	1233.65
8/11	*Theinval, Assam Black, Opening Batsman, Rock On Ruby, Sir Walter Scott, One Pekan	1236.65
7/11	Al Musheer, Dispour, Kilgeel Hill *Wiseton	1243.65
6/11	Separate Shadows, The Backup Plan, Right To Rule * Agent Fedora W4.98, *Tears Of The Sun	1248.65
5/11	Cordite, Mops Angel, Laughing Rock, Tullyesker Hill W5.59, Cracker, Keep In Line, Musaddas W5.7	1245.09
4/11	Pal Ella, Karaka Jack, Nay Secret, Rioja Day, *Ghazi	1241.26
3/11	Utopie Des Bordes, Call The Cops, Bears Affair *Zac Brown *She's Noble	1247.26
2/11	Warriors Tale, Tutchec	1244.28
1/11	Bitter Lake, *Its A Mans World, *Taquin Du Seuil	1246.28
31/10	Keepers Ring, Zynah	1251.28
30/10	Velvet Cognac, L'Amiral David, Faery Song *Tamasha *Gemax	1253.28
29/10	It Must Be FaithW5.94, Nellies Quest, Oscatara, Blurred Lines, Tijan, Missed CallW11.16, Tabjeel, Celestial Knight W9.0	1260.28
28/10	Nortron, Bikini Island *Forza Blacky	1242.33
27/10	Bracka Legend, Kashatree, Harris Tweed	1246.33
25/10	Vieux Lion Rouge ,*Long Lunch,*Bells 'N' Banjos, Fencing, Sky Steps,*Tayma, Law Keeper	1249.33
24/10	*Sylvette, Sleeper King, Norway Cross	1259.33
23/10	KalaneW12.5, Ready Token, *Trapper PeakW27.2, Cultram AbbeyW13.87, Lovely Memory, Hurricane Alert, Muqarred	1263.33
22/10	Wilton Milan, Swallowside, DemographicW9.69, Leoncavallo, Rare RhythmW18.5, *Swordbearer	1195.40
21/10	Emirates Challenge, *Upper StreetW21.0, *Sequester, Beta Tauri, Its A Yes From Me *Ferryview Place	1175.52
20/10	Micras, Invicta Lake W8.21, MarietW8.39	1144.52
19/10	Princess Ombu, Fix It Right	1131.52
18/10	Brick Layer, Carrigeen Lantana,*Autumn Blush W6.27	1133.52
17/10	Charming Thought W39.95, Bracka Legend, Tom Mann, Pulcinella, Mystic Jade,*Humour	1125.52
16/10	Uganda Glory, *Titan Goddess	1094.52
15/10	Magical Thomas,*Double Czech, Engaging Smile, Faery Song, Wild Storm, Ershaadaat, Emirates Joy	1097.52

DATE	WINNERS / LOSERS	TOTAL BFSP
14/10	Desert Ranger, *Justify, Secret Archive, Sabraase, Like A Prayer	1105.52
13/10	**Cosmic RayW 5.74**	1111.52
11/10	Stanarley Pic, Brook, Sivron, Examiner, Rex Imperator, Strong Chemistry, **Lola Montez W3.55**, Todegica	1107.02
10/10	Pillar Box, Asian Trader, **HomageW8.43**, Sun Odyssey, **Little JonW6.86**, *Zac Brown	1110.60
9/10	*El Toreros, Heading Home	1102.97
8/10	**King BoleteW4.11**, *Dame LucyW23.71, Designate, Panatella, Elizona	1105.97
7/10	*Desert Encounter, Dana's Present, **Mister MaydayW6.60**, Right Of Appeal	1061.87
6/10	Festival Theatre, Melvyn The Great	1060.55
5/10	Al Musheer, Swift Arrow	1062.55
4/10	Shagah, Sky Lantern, Viewpoint, *Dream And Hope, Tsarglas, Dukes Delight, Knavery	1064.55
3/10	*Uganda Glory *Tawelya, Artistic Queen, Secret Suspect	1072.55
2/10	Degooch, Vinstar, **Whatdoesthefoxsay W4.1**, *Secret Archive	1078.55
1/10	Hyphaema, Shirleys Pride	1079.60
30/9	Dutch Rifle, Law Keeper, *National Service	1081.60
29/9	Rayak, Bowberry	1085.60
28/9	Finn Class, In Focus, Shot In The Sun *Birdman	1087.60
27/9	Crystal Malt, Misterioso, Light Glass, Mijhaar, Hawker, Candella, Marmalad, **Barracuda Boy W17.84**, Hot Coffee, *Ben Hall	1092.60
26/9	Zibelina, Penglai Pavilion, **Lap Of LuxuryW14.5**, Showing Character, Chosen Character, *Sbrasse W 7.72	1086.60
25/9	Its Gonna Be Me, Regal Missile, Enville, Goal, Little Pop, Azmaam	1065.48
24/9	Be My Gal, Golden Horn, Minight Dance	1070.48
23/9	Resonant,*Swaheen, First Battalion, Remix, Lola Montez, *Winter SpiceW4.64	1073.48
22/9	Missisipi Baileys, Lady Frances, Staffhoss, *Greatest Journey, Gold Will, **Forest MaidenW7.2**, Perfect Alchemy, Invasor Luck, **Killing TimeW12.1**, *Tweedswood	1072.56
21/9	Fighter Jet, Prettyasapicture, Fiasco, Dazzling Rita, Fond Memory, Outbacker	1066.12
20/9	Two For Two, **Earth DrummerW5.07**, International Name, *Fiftyshadesdarker	1072.12
19/9	Tara Muck, Celesta, **Mission To MarsW3.97**, Geordie George, Noble Assett W23.85, Moidore	1072.25
18/9	Temperance Society, Sir Mike, Tachophobia, **SemeenW5.1**, **AnderiegoW6.8**, Parona Ciana, **EvanscentW7.1**, *AlmerzenW8.25	1051.72
17/9	Sir Charlie Kunz, Eleusis	1026.74
16/9	Wu Zetian	1028.74
15/9	Torridonian,*Sky Steps, Pass Muster, Iftikaar	1029.74
13/9	Scoppio Del Carro, Alpine Storm, Winter Spice, Choice Of Destiny, * Mrs Warren	1034.74
12/9	Lahaag, Sir Walter Scott, Loving Home, Bikini Island	1040.74
11/9	Stocking, Criteria, Long Cross, Decorated Knight, Daisy's Secret, **Ancient GreeceW9.7**, Norse Light	1044.74

DATE	WINNERS / LOSERS	TOTAL BFSP
10/9	*Mishko	1042.47
9/9	Alnashama, Master Choice, Flamme Fantastique, Book'em Danno	1044.47
8/9	**High ExpectationsW10.0**, *The Wallace Line, Castorienta, Fiftyshadesofgrey	1048.47
7/9	Royal Mezyan, Jacobs Pillow	1035.37
6/9	Strong Chemistry, Musaddas, Maftool, **NautilusW13.0**, *Reesha, *Kuda Hoora	1037.37
5/9	**Saarrem W9.8**, Tawelya, The Fairy, Tropicana Bay, Cape Of Hope, Cheworee, Deauville Prince, Bold Appeal, Pacific Trip, Mister Mayday, Directional, Gold Waltz	1021.57
4/9	Yazan,*Sky Steps	1024.21
3/9	Ashkari, Bright Cecily, Like A Prayer	1027.21
2/9	*Straighttothepoint, Cosquillas, Potent Embrace, Presto Boy, Swordbearer,*Tamya, Green Monkey,*Taquka	1030.21
1/9	Colours Of Glory,*Picture Postcard, Candlelight	1041.21
31/8	Consortium, Hierach	1045.21
30/8	Asian Trader, Lexington Times, Mount Shamsan, Dungannon, *Vesperal Dream, Strumble Head,*Major Attitude	1047.21
29/8	*Goldcrets, Dittander, Felix De Vega, **Fiftyshadesfreed W3.81**	1056.21
28/8	Relentless Pursuit, Shah Of Persia, Nelson's Pride, Torridon, Jalingo	1054.87
27/8	*Perfect Outcome, *Rembrandt Van Rijn, Red Velour, Evident, It's A Yes From Me, *Forte, *Musaddas	1058.87
26/8	Silver Shuffle, Dutch Rifle	1070.87
25/8	*Vixen Hill, *End Of The Line	1072.87
24/8	Water Thief, King Of Macedon, Right Of Appeal, **Princes's Trust W9.99**	1076.87
23/8	Sir Walter Scott, Dare To Achieve, **Queensbury Rules, W10.5**, Royal Mezyan	
	Katchapoly, Hooded, Lizzie Tudor, Cameron Highland	1071.33
22/8	Semeen, Satellite, Ertijaal, Foreign Diplomat, **White LakeW40.0**, Perfect Pursuasion Indian Champ, Soul Instinct, **Swivel W 6.45**,* Hiking	1069.30
21/8	**Mubtaghaa W12.42**, Valley Of Fire, **Queen Of Ice W27.0**, Sweet Charlie	1036.07
20/8	Mukhadram, Roossey, Stopped Out, Entihaa, Rocky Two, *Prince Of Islay, Gay Marriage, *Hill Battles, *Moonlight Venture, Incredible Fresh, Invasor Luck, Furos	1002.52
19/8	*Mambo Rhythm, Patronella,*Picture Postcard, *El Toreros	1017.52
18/8	**Wahgah W8.8**, *Romance Story, Keeper's Ring, *Designate	1024.52
17/8	**West End W2.52**,* Dealing River, Survived, Oxsana	1022.11
16/8	Tendu, Billy Blue, **ChellallaW10.0**, *Velator	1023.22
15/8	*Too The Stars, Nagambie	1010.12
14/8	*Twin Turbo, Overclear, **JewelleryW 3.45, Lost EchoW3.85**	1013.12
13/8	Arthurs Melody, Prince Of Time, Power Up, *Bartholomew Fair, Anton Chigurh, **Venus Marina W4.26**	1011.08
12/8	*Rasselas, *Curbyourenthusiasm, *Secret Spirit, *Sioux Chieftain, Lola Montez, *Super Moment, S**equester W 5.7**	1013.98

DATE	WINNERS / LOSERS	TOTAL BFSP
10/8	*Dinneratmidnight	1020.51
9/8	**Squats W4.4**, Queensbury Rules, Lahaag, Solar Magic, Provident Spirit, **CornrowW5.7**, Elsiniaar, Satellite	1022.51
8/8	**KhelmanW12.63**, Just Paul, Rocky Two, *Laurelita, *Muzarkash, *Idder,* Red Velour	1020.81
7/8	*Cayjo, *Hoop Of Colour	1019.76
6/8	Renaissant, *Heho, Arbaab	1023.76
5/8	*Escrick, Swan Lakes, **Momayyaz W5.57,** Swordbearer	1027.76
4/8	*Allegation, *Warfare, Celestial Knight, **TacheeW4.5**, *Desert Command	1027.42
3/8	IntransigentW13.0, **RoskillyW5.5**, Unforgettable	1031.09
2/8	Huntsmans Close, *Allegria, An Chulainn	1016.41
1/8	Blurred Lines, Herecomesthebride, **Giovanni Jack W10.83**, Cara's Request, Smart Alec Spellbind	1020.41
31/7	Endless Credit	1016.07
30/7	***Magique W36.91**, Observational, Hiking, Winter Music, Carlanstown	1017.07
29/7	Manshaa, **Special Fighter W2.5**, Explained, Seismic, Drunken Council	952.84
28/7	*Lola Montez, *Little Buxted	955.41
26/7	**Muthmir W5.7**, **Valley Of Fire W5.92**, Pillar Box, *The Gold Cheongsam	959.31
25/7	***Orion's Bow W6.2**	953.17
24/7	Red Perdita, ***Purple Spectrum W7.64**, **Synergise W7.14**, Khatiba, *Westminster, *My Target, *Thataboy	943.29
23/7	*Saarrem	931.84
22/7	Ixelles Diamond	933.84
21/7	Lightnin Hopkins, Corncockle, Dubai Hills, **Mr Satco W4.86**, Nodform Richard, Dunowen Point, Majestic Manner	934.84
20/7	Maxi Chop, Vujiyama	937.18
19/7	Long Cross, Deuce Again, Pillar Box, Discoverie, **Cool Baranca W6.2**, Rocksee	939.18
18/7	Endless Seas, Khajaaly, Tony Hollis, Double Up, The Character, Bonnie Charlie Layla's Hero, **Blaine W7.2**, Double Bluff, Stout Cortez, Keep To The Beat, Rasselas, Zac Brown, **Jamesbo's Girl W5.8**	939.24
17/7	**Another Lincolnday W18.33,* Secular Society W6.98**	939.79
16/7	*Gran Maestro, **Mick Duggan W4.8**	911.96
15/7	*Potent Embrace, **Orlando Rogue W3.9**, Semaral, Venus Marina, Roring Samson	910.35
14/7	Tarvini, Ubaldo Des Mehnies, *Powerful Presence, *Thataboy, *Tabjeel, *Perfect Outcome, *Emirates Challenge, **Rekdhat W8.44**	908.10
13/7	CygnetW3.65, Mr Bricolage, Stormbay Bomber	913.03
12/7	Queensbury Rules, **Commanchero W9.0**, Bapak Muda	912.51
11/7	*Survived, *Perfect Mission, *Zeshov	906.91
10/7	**Water Hole W6.0**, Outback Ruler, Winter Spice	912.91
9/7	Authorized Too, *Petticoat Lane, **Aomen Rock W7.92**, Zman Awal, *Bowie Boy, *Impressive Victory, *Almanack, **EmulatringW8.95**	910.16
8/7	*Eloquence, *Noble Descent, Roring Samson, Society Diva	906.03
7/7	Poolstock, Powerful Presence, Pimm Street, *Grey Blue , Amuse Me	912.03

DATE	WINNERS / LOSERS	TOTAL BFSP
5/7	*Carnevale	918.03
4/7	Sejel, Algeria, Celestial Vision, *No One Knows W4.07, Stec W46.0,* Quasqazah, The Character, Showstoppa, King Of Macedeon, Loud ,Mitchelton, Enquiring	920.03
3/7	All Reddy, Faydhan W2.06, Little Belter, Joshua Potman, W5.9, Hunters Creek, Seismic ,Winter Music, Pumped Up Kicks W6.01, Moss Street, Lady Mia, Dolorous ,Stella Bellissima W6.29, Purple Spectrum, Fastnet Red, Elpida	880.45
2/7	*Alphabetical Order, Lady Fingers, *Champion Versions, With A Twist, *Almanack W24.39, Romance Story, Expert FighterW4.7	876.00
1/7	Rookery, Mambo Rhythm, Locky Taylor, Hopes And DreamsW4.85, Castorienta, Melburn Cutler, Sherston, *Red Lady W8.25	835.23
30/6	Midaz, *Intrepid, *Boy In The Bar W7.4, *Lady Sparkler, *Sir Rosco	823.80
29/6	Jazz ManW2.96	824.72
28/6	Desert Law	822.86
27/6	Bahamian C W7.8, *Secular Society, Nonno Giulio, Queens Dream	823.86
26/6	Heartbreak Hero, Emerald Sea, Redkirk W8.29, *Dynaglow, First Move, Pigeon Pie, Greenhead High, Cape Of Hope, Bonnie Charlie	821.40
25/6	*What A Jewel, Musaddas, Furas, *Rathaath W2.82, Enquiring W12.5, Special Fighter Invincible Wish, Dodina , Penina	823.47
24/6	Power Up, AyralW5.6, *Gabriel The Terror W 6.38, All Rounder, Gay Marriage	817.09
23/6	Cape Victoria, Comanchero, *Calamity Jane, *L'EtacqW2.44, Certificate W3.35, PannetoneW8.27, Femme De Menage , Classical Art W3.2	805.50
22/6	Caius College Girl	796.53
21/6	Classic Flyer, Jaahiez	797.53
20/6	Vinnie My Boy, Book Em DannoW3.82, Temptress, Why Not Now	799.53
19/6	Miss Acclaimed,Musical MollyW 11.0, *Hit The Lights	799.85
18/6	Bapak Muda,Handwoven, Sir Guy PorteuosW5.5, Swehan	794.30
17/6	Don Padeja W7.0, Steady Major, Desert Ace W10.05	793.02
16/6	Vodka Wells, Make On madamW4.1, Go Sakhee W5.87, IgidereW3.87	779.72
15/6	*Idder	770.42
14/6	Kyllachy Star, Pass Muster, Ballesteros, Fury, Royal Mezyan, Zaraee	772.42
13/6	Grace And Favour, Dandy W6.01, Perfect Mission, Dreaming Beauty	778.42
11/6	Allgeria W7.2, Staffhoss ,Cayjo, Enquiring, Mountain Dew, Torridon	776.66
10/6	What A Jewel, Vodka N' Tonic, *Foggy's Wall, OverclearW20.0	775.77
8/6	Vasco Du Mee W1.89, Ghost River W 3.37	761.72
7/6	Diamond Creek	758.62
6/6	Madame Chiang, Momentus	759.62
5/6	*Come On Dave, *Deep Resolve, *Grandest, *Desert Snow, *Bowie Boy, *Don't Stare, Greenhead High, Layla's Hero	761.62
4/6	Milgen Bay, *New Horizons, Robinsson, *Intrepid, *Frankthetank W1.94, *Highplains Drifter, Swordbearer, Tahchee	775.62
3/6	*Adaay W1.88, *Wistar W3.8, *Mccarthy Mor	784.83
2/6	*Tap Your Toes, Red Velour, Scoppio Del Carro, *Alaskan Bullet	779.84

DATE	WINNERS / LOSERS	TOTAL BFSP
31/5	**Sultanina W15.33**, Eton Forever, **Steps W9.25**, Classical Art, Purcell, Storm Force Ten, *Muradif, ***Chase The Wind W2.46**, *Fastnet Red	785.84
30/5	*Opera Fan, Oscar Prairie, **Paint The CloudsW2.62**, *Maljaa, **Snap Shots W2.97**, Mount Shamsan, Day Dreamer, **Agent Murphy W50.0**, Vilaz	769.61
29/5	Chosen Character, **Aldwick Bay W3.3**, *Shades Of Grey	727.65
28/5	*Secret Beau, ***AldboroughW4.14**, Delores Rocket, **Zanouska,W6.10**, Mac's Superstar, He's My Boy, Aomen Rock	728.46
25/5	*Golden Hoof, *Roberto Goldbac, *Lyric Street,	723.65
24/5	Danzili Lane, **Bear Behind W19.5**, Hot Coffee, Bilimbi, **Wrangler W2.11**	729.65
23/5	***Johara W2.42**, ***Observational W2.96**, ***Campelopardalis W3.05**, **Crowleys Law W3.81**, **Elusive Epona W3.0**, *Arthur Mc Bride	714.02
22/5	Inoogoo, So Beloved, Skilled	703.08
21/5	**Vesperal Dream W1.66**, Vide Cave, ***Dreams Of Reality W10.0**, Shushu Sugartown, ***Magic Hurricane W3.95**, Sergeant Thunder W5.7, **Merrion Square W3.25**	706.08
20/5	*Alketios	678.15
19/5	Diamond Gesture, Darting, Ballygroonbie, **Bertie W15.36**	680.15
18/5	Mission Complete, Tenmoku, **Book'em Danno W5.5**	668.51
17/5	Brass Ring,Angelic Air, Ballybriggan, **Whatdoesthefoxsay W4.2**, Madame De Guise	666.23
16/5	Likelihood, Simple Magic, Layla's Hero	667.19
15/5	**Takeyourcapoff W7.2**,* Fury	680.19
14/5	Queen Of Ice, Heerat, For Two	677.30
13/5	**Busatto W10.35, Dry Your EyesW6.4**, Quinsman	680.30
12/5	Fallen In Line, Nothing Special, Lola Galli, Bishophill Jack, **Cloughernagh Boy W 4.4**, *Out Of Bounds	667.29
10/5	*Saigon City, George Benjamin	670.06
9/5	Theatrelands, Chain Of Beacons, Century, **Kingfisher W3.8**	673.06
8/5	*Morito Du Berlais, Romsdal, *Talkin Thomas	673.40
7/5	Anglo Irish, *Intermedium	678.40
6/5	**Mac's Superstar W6.2**, Dubai Hadeia, Don't Stare, Billingsgate	681.40
5/5	Golden Hoof, Parish Business, Opera Fan	679.46
3/5	B**e My Gal W8.8, TemptressW12.77**	682.46
2/5	Reverb, Requin, Lady Of Provence , *Georgie Lad	663.87
1/5	West End, Taffy Dare, **Crazy Jack W14.52**, Sparville, Bishophill Jack	667.87
29/4	Drifter, Rocksee, Yeager	659.03
28/4	Wall Street Boss, Aomen Rock, *Rocket Ship	661.03
26/4	*Comedy King, Cash And Go, Vasco Du Ronceray	665.03
25/4	Votary, Munatas, Five Star Wilsham,*Top Wood	669.03
24/4	Hollow Blue Sky	674.03
23/4	Flying Eagle, **Lamboro Lad W 6.95**, Church Bray, *Rocky Bender, **Kings Grey W6.0**, Donna's Pride	675.03
22/4	Fearless Tunes, Hollow Tree, **Keeneland W5.45**, Laughing Jack, ***Sir Mike W4.0**	669.63
21/4	*Westminster, Artifice Sivola	662.70

DATE	WINNERS / LOSERS	TOTAL BFSP
20/4	Here Now And Why, **Pass Muster W11.71**, King Muro, Counting House	**665.70**
19/4	Designate, **Seaside SizzlerW7.96**, Shooters Wood, Lady Fingers	**658.53**
16/4	Handwoven, **Blue Atlantic DH 4.79**, Emaad, Beylerbey, Dynamic Vision, Emirati Spirit, Toofi, Ayrad	**654.92**
15/4	**Miss Ballantyne W8.8, Realize W7.9**, Aiyana	**660.12**
14/4	Colonel Mak, Newstead Abbey	**647.15**
13/4	*Stevie Thunder	**649.15**
12/4	Master Butcher, Crowd Control,Fortrose Academy, Gallic Destiny	**651.15**
11/4	**Kasb W11.94**, Ski Lift, Wojha, **Bright Approach W4.3**, Criteria, *Role Reversal	**656.15**
10/4	*Early Bonnett, Playhara, **Hel Tara W4.08**	**647.62**
9/4	Grandest, Passionate Affair, Saarrem, *Invasor Luck, Witch From Rome	**647.69**
8/4	*Ko Cache, ***Deep Resolve W3.95**	**653.69**
7/4	Whiskey Chaser, *Gone With The Wind, Good Value	**650.08**
6/4	Grey Blue,Madame De Guise, **Spartan Angel W3.53**, Titchwood, Touch Back	**654.08**
5/4	Twin Point, The Firm , Milor De La Borie, *Secret Suspect	**655.68**
4/4	*Daneglow, *Regal Selection	**660.68**
3/4	*Designate, Don Sigfredo, Quamtum Dot	**664.68**
2/4	*Serena Grae,* I'm Super Too, *Arctic Moon, Mountain Dew	**668.68**
1/4	*Mr Shantu, My Boy Paddy, Aldborough, Last Echo	**675.68**
29/3	*Red Seventy, ***Crystal Lake W8.52**, Fencing, Romsdal, Leader Of The Gang, **Molo W6.08**	**680.68**
28/3	*Villoresi, Rayak	**666.57**
27/3	Zamra, *Ubaldo Des Menhies	**669.57**
26/3	Goodlukin Lucy	**672.57**
25/3	Tiller Belle, *Red Rock, Moulin De La Croix, Exitas	**673.57**
24/3	Very Noble, *Mink Coat	**678.57**
23/3	*Wyoyo, **Book'em Danno W5.5**, *Maestro Royal, Rons Dream	**681.57**
22/3	**Keenland W14.5**, Sydney Padget, Hellorboston, Plan Again, ***Watt Broderick W2.96**, Court Room, *Sea Here, Nautilus	**678.02**
21/3	*The Firm, ***Muhdiq W4.83**	**668.47**
20/3	*Makadamia, Hallouella, Zamra, *Benandonner	**664.19**
18/3	*Interior Minister, Sky Ranger	**670.19**
17/3	*Role Reversal	**673.19**
16/3	Vermouth Bleu, Carlton Jack, Titchwood	**675.19**
15/3	HollowTree, RightTo Rule, Golden Hoof, Top Of The Range, Ryde By Knight, **GoulanesW8.44**	**678.19**
14/3	Ujagar, Mahadee, *Frederic Chopin, *Limon Squeezy	**676.11**
13/3	*Castorienta, ***Genius Boy W1.72**	**681.11**
12/3	*Trefnant, *Taquka	**681.74**
11/3	***Dividend Dan W3.35**	**685.74**
10/3	***Our Phylli Vera W2.32**, Mandy's Boy, **Sonofagun W6.53**	**681.27**
8/3	Requin, Bertiewhittle, Fourth Estate, Side Step	**674.51**
7/3	**In Fairness W9.2**, Willpower	**678.51**
5/3	**Waltzing Darling W5.6**,* Arabian Heights	**671.72**

DATE	WINNERS / LOSERS	TOTAL BFSP
4/3	Tatting	669.35
3/3	*Club House, *Izbushka	670.35
1/3	Ballista, Castillo Del Diablo, Smadynium, Franciscan	674.35
28/2	Windlass, **Menelik W4.6**, WhisperingStar, **BenHall W3.73**, ***SpesNostraW4.2**, *Hustle Bustle	678.35
27/2	Fort Belvedere	666.84
26/2	The Boss Of Me, Radebe	667.84
25/2	Orlittlebylittle, Welsh Bard, Egypt Mill Spirit	669.84
24/2	Rocky Stone, Sorry Saeed, **Desert Ranger W6.33**, *Dividend Dan	672.84
22/2	**Buddy Bolero W14.67, Poole Master W6,74**, Anaconda, Cup Final	671.78
21/2	Alderluck , Western Diva	655.34
20/2	Primary Route, *Kickingthelilly, Tom Mann	657.34
19/2	Shakalakaboomboom, *Last Echo	661.34
18/2	Take The Lead, Greenhead High, Torgamah lad	664.34
17/2	*Doctor Parkes	667.34
15/2	*Birdman	669.34
14/2	*Experimentalist, Hawkes Point, **Commissar W9.6**	671.34
12/2	**Shannon Haven W23.35**, (DH) Radio Nowhere, Darlington County, Kitchapoly	658.00
11/2	*Nubar Boy, **Arr' KidW3.03**, Beautiful StrangerW7.04	649.91
10/2	Diocles, Short Takes	644.24
9/2	*Hint Of Mint	646.24
8/2	***Tullyesker Hill W3.8**	648.24
7/2	Albert Bridge, *Valdaw	642.92
6/2	One Conemara, Union Du Chenet	645.92
5/2	*Labise	647.92
4/2	Josie's Dream, Angelo Poliziano, Imperial Spirit, ***Abi Scarlet W11.5**, *Warbrook, *Taffy Thomas	649.92
3/2	*Golden Calf,* Daneglow	636.97
2/2	Clondaw Hero, Witness In Court, Franciscan, Sud Pacifique	640.97
1/2	Smoking Aces, Kaikias, ***Swiss Cross W12.66**, Stevie Thunder	644.97
31/1	*Alderley Rover	625.82
30/1	***Gogeo W6.7**	627.82
29/1	***Bapak Pesta W3.95**, Taquka	622.40
28/1	Exmoor Mist	617.79
27/1	*Aramadyh	618.79
25/1	Hidden Justice, **Master Of The Game W20.42**	620.79
24/1	Menelik, Accordingtojodie, *Severiano, *Nasijah	603.34
23/1	*Franklin Roosevelt, Mister Manannan	609.34
22/1	Jump Up, *Santo Thomas, Grape Tree Flame, ***Gone With The Wind W2.8**	612.34
21/1	Investment Expert, *Tiller Belle	612.92
20/1	Kellys Eye	615.92
18/1	The Minack, Sydney Padget, Vasco Pierji	616.92

DATE	WINNERS / LOSERS	TOTAL BFSP
17/1	*Nubar Boy, *Honest Strike, *Mersad, **Cloudante W13.72**, Sud Pacifique, Stoming Gale	619.92
15/1	Izbushka	615.84
13/1	*Present Trend, Rocky Bender, ***Compton W 3.7**	616.84
11/1	Josses Hill, Rover Maigue, Nadiya De La Vega, **Lyvius W 3.57**, Bygones Sovereign, Master Overseer	617.27
10/1	**Stanlow W7.98**, *Ptolemy	619.83
9/1	*Precariously Good, *Bint Malyana , Sealous Scout, Smadynium, Welsh Bard	615.20
8/1	*Wiki Tiki, ***Nubar Boy W14.69**, Act Alone W5.3	622.20
7/1	Whats Happening, Egypt Mill Spirit	594.10
6/1	Blue Oyster, ***Secret Suspect W15.0**, Choice Of Destiny	596.10
5/1	Kellys Eye	571.50
4/1	**Knockgraffon King W4.58**, My Kingdom	572.50
2/1	Vasco Pierji , ***Global Explorer W3.3**	570.10
1/1/14	Divers, Riguez Dancer, The Backup Plan , Short Takes, Iayl, Tax Free	566.73
31/12	*Menelik, Notus De La Tour	571.73
30/12	***Thataboy W5.1**, *Favourite Treat, *Veratan, **Across The Bay W11.6**	574.73
29/12	Sound Investment, **Mister Dillon W10.73**, Nesterenko W10.52, *Bapak Sayang	560.87
28/12	Blessington, Benzanno, Tullyesker Hill, Exmoor Mist, **Le Rocher W8.6**	545.58
27/12	Touch Back, Utopie Des Bordes	542.36
26/12	**Kings Grace W4.73**, *Billybo, Vaniteux, McIlhatton, Lifetime , Grouse Lodge, Right To Rule, **Spanish Arch W4.2**, Mirror	544.36
22/12	Irish Tears, El Macca	545.78
21/12	Smadynium, Tonvadosa, Forever Present, Cedre Bleu, Galaician, Perivale	547.78
20/12	Bapak Pesta, Keep To The Beat, Polly Peachum, *Libra Romana	553.78
19/12	Jalingo, Silly Billy, Volt Face, Jigsaw Puzzle	558.78
18/12	***Welease Bwian W9.09**, **Betimes W4.45**, Outbacker, Nimiety, **Benvolio W10.07**, Poungach ,*Mercury Magic	562.78
17/12	*Hot Stock, Whichwaytobougie	540.51
16/12	Aqua Ardens, *Rally, Gate Please, **Imagine The Chat W3.68**, Titchwood, Ubaldo Des Menhies, ***Our Phyllivera W6.31**	543.51
15/12	*In The Gate, *Squeeze Me	537.87
14/12	Howelongisafoot, Woodbank ,Empire Levant, Ranjaan, Bears Affair, Harry The Viking, *Excel Best, Newsreader, **Dame Nellie Melba W13.5**, *Libra Roma, *Valdaw	541.87
13/12	Samoset	542.99
12/12	Supreme Assett , Radio Knowhere, Redkalani, Springinherstep, Nordic Quest	543.99
9/12	*Turnbury, *Mairise, Katachenko, ***Discussiontofollow W5.4**	548.99
8/12	Sud Pacifique, **Kruzhlinin W5.6**, Ulzana's Raid	545.63
7/12	Clarence Beeks, Roudoudou Ville, Exmoor Mist, Know More Oats, **Vaniteux W5.0**, Urbain De Sivola	543.26
6/12	Miss Ballantyne, Blessington , Alto Des Mottes	544.46

DATE	WINNERS / LOSERS	TOTAL BFSP
5/12	Shareni , **Bucks Bond W5.6**	547.46
4/12	**Smadynium W6.0**, Star In Flight, Ballyhollow	544.09
3/12	Celtic Abbey, Pampanito	541.34
2/12	*Wiggins	543.34
1/12	Mr Selby, **Tutchec W5.2**, Tiny Dancer , Take A Bow	545.34
30/11	Saphir Du Rheu, Bint Malyana W11.0	544.35
29/11	Cedre Bleu, Tagrita, Fascino Rustico, Woodbank, Black Cow, Rhymers Stone	535.85
28/11	*Lady Fingers, Broomfield, Irish Saint, Foxtrot Jubilee	541.85
27/11	Jalingo	546.85
26/11	*Uppercut De L'Orne, *Fieldgunner Kirkup , *Mill I Am	547.85
25/11	*Forever Present	553.85
24/11	Vintage Vixon, *Revouge	555.85
23/11	Clondaw Kaempfer, **Sydney Paget W7.6** , *Funding Deficit	558.85
22/11	Fransiscan, **Black Thunder W5.3**, Classic Move, **Varom Desoto County W5.0**, Brinestine	555.58
21/11	In The Gate, Spanish Arch , Sound Investment	551.69
20/11	*Thataboy, Penny Sixpence , Blessington , Shady Lane, Madame De Guise, Our Pollyanna, You'resomedreamer ,*Emulating, ***Secret Archive W8.08**	554.69
19/11	Which Way Went, Delores Rocket, **Big Storm Coming W7.0**, *Ioannou, Mill I Am	551.24
18/11	Our Phylli Vera	550.54
15/11	Sweet P, *Rochester, *Eton Dorney, *Excel Best, Alexanor, *Old Town Boy, Koos	551.54
14/11	*Sky Ranger, Kings Lodge, Hare In A Round, Will Power, Sin Bin, Irving W4.5, Mr Bridger	562.54
13/11	Beau De Tabel, Royale's Charter,* Unefille De Guye, *Jalingo, *Desert Skies, *Malt Master, Azure Fly, ***Furas W4.2**	566.21
12/11	Atlanta Falcon	571.13
11/11	Spiculas, Mountain Lion, **Elite Army W6.44**, Classic Devotion, ***Wall Street Boss W5.0**	572.13
10/11	*Abnaki , Little Chip, Greenlaw	562.36
9/11	Be Definite, Ballyallia Man, **Kruzhlinin W6.2**, **Swift Arrow W6.2**, Magistral	566.36
8/11	***Hopeand W6.2**, *Moortahan	559.48
7/11	Uncle Fred, **Scottish Glen W5.8**, Waverunner, **Cloudy Joker W5.9**, Hollow Penny, Amazing D'Azy, *** Prince Alzain W6.0**	551.60
6/11	*Mountain Fighter, Norse Light, *Qalinas, *Mics Delight, **Guess Again W4.8**, Makadamia, Sequester, Entitlement	536.88
4/11	***AnthenianW5.8**, *Rio's Pearl	539.66
1/11	*Lookout Mountain, Tara Muck, *La Belle Epoque,*Choice Of Destiny	532.54
31/10	*Amigo, *Rondeau, ***Killing Time W5.7**, *Mighty Ambition	539.54
30/10	*Houston Dynimo, *Aomen Rock	536.61
29/10	*Magique, *Funding Deficit, *Earthflight	540.61
26/10	**Thomas Hobson W6.6**	546.61

DATE	WINNERS / LOSERS	TOTAL BFSP
25/10	*Louis Ludwig	535.97
24/10	*Speedfit Boy, *You Look So Good, Wall Street Boss, *Lyric Piece	537.97
23/10	*Mighty Mambo, *Simply A Legend, **Black Thunder W4.2**, *Heronry, *Rockweiller	544.97
22/10	*Blossom Lane, *Red Passiflora, **Sweet P W4.40**	546.89
21/10	**Vital Evidence W 6.2**	544.43
20/10	*Gerrards Cross, *Cool Macavity	534.55
19/10	*Namely, *Napinda	538.55
18/10	*Alwilda, *Sunset Shore	542.55
17/10	*Szabo's Art, **Jump City DH 5.0**, *Tae Kwon Do,* Montaigne	546.55
16/10	*Club House	548.75
15/10	**Tweed W3.9**, Trapeze, *Mombasa	550.75
14/10	**Idea W5.3**	548.24
12/10	**Greek Spirit W4.4**, *Daneglow	540.07
11/10	**Earthflight W8.95**, *Mizyen	535.61
9/10	*Melrose Abbey, *Stellar Express, *Stormbay Bomber	522.50
8/10	**Manipulation W5.1**, * Arabian Beauty, *Blossom Lane, *Sky Ranger, *Lyric Street, **Arzag W9.86**	528.50
4/10	**Kings Lodge W3.51**, *Reminisce	511.98
3/10	*Black Vale, **Shyron W6.65**, *Man Of Law	509.21
2/10	Thereabouts, Red Tulip	502.47
1/10	St Vincent, **Port Monarch W5.4**	504.47
29/9	**Just Paul W6.6**	501.29
28/9	Good Speech, *Dick Bos	490.65
27/9	*Hare In A Round,* Napinda, *Red Invader	493.65
26/9	*Soviet Courage, **Bazing Knight W9.31**	499.65
25/9	*Masquerading, *Deserted	493.76
24/9	*Captain Kelly,*Al Freej, **Welease Bwian W6.0**, **Canadian Run W13.79**	497.76
22/9	*Purple N Gold	467.96
21/9	*Threetimesalady, *Mukhabarat	469.96
20/9	**Free Spin W6.0**	473.96
19/9	*Aomen Rock, Perfect Haven, Pompei, *Ikhtisas	464.46
18/9	*Jake's Destiny, Magique, *Typhon, *Wedding Speech, *Hidden Belief	470.46
14/9	*Bravestar, *Killing Time	479.46
13/9	*Camborne W 6.0, **General Miller W 8.92**	483.46
12/9	*Hipster, *Mukhabarat, *Simple Joys, *Don Ottavio	458.91
11/9	*First In The Queue, **Diamonds Return W 20.0**, *Red Tulip, **Justineo W6.6**	466.91
9/9	* Lucilla	424.17
8/9	**Wooly Bully W5.0**, *My Inspiration	426.17
7/9	Clowance Estate, Swiss Spirit, *Exceed Areeda, *Work Ethic, *Juvenal, *Secret Beau	420.57
4/9	*Dama De La Noche, *Hodgson, Perfect Haven	430.57
3/9	Ultimate Warrior, Secret Applause, Camatini, Fair Flutter, Jawaad, Brunello, Diamond Mine, Mawaqeet, Waterlock	435.57

DATE	WINNERS / LOSERS	TOTAL BFSP
2/9	*Feel The Heat W12.5	444.57
1/9	Rum And Butter, My Mate Vinnie, *Gabriels Gift W4.5	422.72
31/8	Enrol, Bailys Jubilee, Copperwood, Ibecke	418.07
30/8	Haayil, Yenhaab, Snow Powder, Empress Adelaide, *Regal Silk, Handsome Stranger,	422.07
29/8	Wellingrove W7.8*, Safe Investment W6.8, Wave The Grapes, Red Tulip W5.0, *Lightening Spear W 6.8, Quality Alliance	429.07
28/8	*Portrait, Castle Beach, Ehtedaam W6.0, *Emilio Largo, Hidden Belief, *Fluctuation, Hunting Ground W11.0, Secretori	397.82
27/8	Seperate Shadows	385.87
26/8	*Ellalan, Hipster, Fraserburgh, Baltic Gin	386.87
25/8	Bourbon, Overstep, Shagwa, Circus Turn W15.5	391.87
24/8	Ghazi W5.4, Outback Traveller, Tahaamah, Langley House, Oh Right, More Equity W6.0, Bright Abbey, Thistle Bird, *Modern Tutor W5.5, Gallipot	381.09
23/8	Our Jonathan, Gramercy W12.5, Twirling Magnet, Night Party, Istikshaf,	370.61
22/8	Nezar, Haikbidiac W12.0, Lightening Shower, *Quintet W 7.92	363.68
21/8	Platinum W4.0, Just Paul	342.08
20/8	North Pole W 4.0, *Marju's Quest W3.8, Percythepinto	340.23
19/8	Flew The Nest, On The Off Chance, *Mocacha, Proximate, * Al jamal W 4.51	333.06
17/8	Lost In The Moment, Royal EmpireW 7.8, Tawhid, *Strumble Head W5.6	331.39
16/8	Elnadwa, *Grass Green,* Excuse To Linger, *Kickboxer	318.19
15/8	Safe Investment, Baltic Gin, *Nellie Forbush	325.19
14/8	Full Day, *Gone Dutch W5.8, Hidden Belief	329.19
13/8	*Itmakessense, Basil Fawlty, Muntasir	322.07
12/8	Zampa Manos W 9.95, Black Cadillac	326.07
11/8	*Fotrinbrass, Red Refraction	318.57
10/8	Danchai, *Sri Putra, Dare To Achieve	321.57
9/8	*The Great Gabriel W5.8, *Phiz W5.2, *Mimbleberry	325.57
6/8	Rio's Pearl	310.47
5/8	Centrality, Sleek, Duchess Of Seville	311.47
4/8	First Flight W5.31, Palkin, Get Home Now W5.79, Vinnie My Boy	314.47
3/8	Strange Magic, Hopes N Dreams W5.17, Wellingrove, King Kurt	307.82
2/8	Manchestar W 7.6, Chloe's Image, Just Paul W 4.42	306.86
1/8	Lucky To Be Alive, Royal PeakW16.1, *Astra Hall W18.0, Fortinbrass W5.34, Hipster	298.34
31/7	Faiwood Massini W4.7, Terfel's Tosca W12.55, *Stars Above Me, Thomas Hobson W6.09, Enharmonic	249.57
30/7	*Excuse To Linger W5.3, Cap Eleron W7.24, Silver Lime, Clowance Estate, Captain Cat, *Mumbles Head W4.0	233.25
29/7	*Gold Mine	216.45
27/7	Stalactite, Greek War, Mar Mar	218.45
26/7	*Laustra Bad, Solicitation	221.45
25/7	Willowing	224.45

DATE	WINNERS / LOSERS	TOTAL BFSP
24/7	Safe Investment, **Menelik W6.16**	225.45
23/7	**Green Bank W9.14**, Kings Destiny, An Capall Mor, The Weatherman, **Brigadoon W 4.0**	221.55
22/7	**Seargent Pink W7.8**, The Wizard Of Aus, The Moaning Butcher	213.97
21/7	Strumble Head	209.51
20/7	**Mr Satco W6.71**, Dineur, **General Miller W8.3, Snowboarder W8.51**, Shelley's Choice, Switcherooney	210.51
19/7	Music Theory, Thataboy, Turin, **Investment Expert W14.0**, Mount Logan	194.02
18/7	Thurayaat, *Lady Vermeer	185.67
17/7	**Purple N Gold W4.95**,* Basford Ben, Cap Elorn W7.43, Brough Academy	188.67
16/7	***About Turn W4.0, *W9.21**	177.06
15/7	*Polisky, **Trading Profit W3.48**, *Moaning Butcher	155.76
14/7	Faiwood Massini, Karinga Queen, **Dineur 3.64**	157.40
13/7	Guarantee, **Danchai W12.0**, Stencive, Dakota Canyon	156.89
12/7	Majestic Red, Restiadargent, Fire Blaze	149.44
11/7	Mariners Moon, Tarikhi, Fantastic Moon	152.44
10/7	*Harbinger Lass	155.44
9/7	*Tussie Mussie	157.44
8/7	Black Cadillac, ***Nezar W8.2**	159.44
7/7	Cape Express	146.76
6/7	***Sandy's Row 8.82, Ashaad 5.4**, Cappa Rosso,	147.76
5/7	*The Kid, *Playbill	129.72
4/7	Mr Satco, *Saddaqa, **Hot Coffee W10.05**	133.72
3/7	Trend Is My Friend, D J Milan, **Dantes King W38.0**, Latest Trend, The Weatherman, **Seal Of Approval W16.43, Bailey Storm W18.1, Divine Folly W19.28**, *One Lucky Lady	128.12
2/7	***The Strig W5.25**, Icendo, **Overstep W36.0**, Grandiloquent, Beacon Lodge, **Galician W 8.3**, True That, **Imperial Legend W8.83**	50.70
1/7	Chinese Jade	-1